Tandra,
keep connecting
with intuition!

Best
Molly
11·2016

THE NETWORKED
ORGANIZATION

Published in the United States by
Studio C
www.gostudioc.com

Editing and Book Design by
Harvard Girl Word Services
www.heidiconnolly.com

For information about special discounts for bulk purchases, please contact info@mollywendell.com.

Library of Congress Control Number 2015912550
ISBN 978-0-9966762-0-5
ISBN 978-0-9966762-5-0 (pbk)

PRINTED IN THE UNITED STATES OF AMERICA
10 9 8 7 6 5 4 3 2 1

THE NETWORKED ORGANIZATION

MOLLY WENDELL

DEDICATION

To Mom: You taught me the golden rule of networking at such a young age. You have always made it about everyone but you. You're great with names and faces. You meet people, remember people, and figure out how to help or connect people more than anyone I know. Thank you for imparting such an incredible life lesson to me!

To my husband Tom: Thank you for all those nights and weekends where you took on kid duty so I could have the time and space to write this book. Your input on and willingness to practice my networking techniques, as well as your commitment to reviewing chapter after chapter—again and again, was invaluable. Writing this was definitely more difficult than having twins, but your support made it that much easier. Thank you for helping get my passion in print.

And to Sammy: I love you with all my heart.

Acknowledgments

I'd like to say thank you to the following for their help in making this book a reality. Whether through inspiration or direct effort, you have all made this book what it is today.

To God, Who gave me the gift of networking and Who guides me always.

To my editor Heidi Connolly, who helped me understand what role a really good editor plays.

To Jackie Werner, one of my "oldest" friends, who did a great job taking my content and turning it into infographics.

To Dale Carnegie, who essentially initiated the conversation on building relationships, one that remains as relevant today as it was in the 1930s.

To Malcolm Gladwell, who introduced the importance of connectors in *The Tipping Point*.

To Keith Ferrazzi, who motivated the world to think about connecting on a deeper level to create a more meaningful life.

To the executives in Executives Network who have open ears when it comes to my networking strategies and suggestions.

To my clients for proving the point that great business relationships can result from an airplane ride.

To my family, who has always supported me in everything I do.

To all those other authors who have never failed to inspire me, especially C. K. Prahalad, Gary Hamel, Stephen M. R. Covey, Michael Porter, Dewitt Jones, Arthur Hailey, Michael Treacy, and Fred Weirsema.

TABLE OF CONTENTS

FOREWORD

BY KEITH FERRAZZI

I've built my company, Ferrazzi Greenlight, on the foundation that our success as individuals and organizations is directly related to the strength of our networks. For years now, I've spoken and written about this topic extensively. As a working-class kid from Youngstown, PA, I wouldn't have been able to accomplish a fraction of what I've done in my life without the great family, friends, and mentors in my life, all of whom have helped make me the man I am today.

Technology, however, has changed the game. While technology has made it easier to be more connected than ever, it has also supported us in having and developing weaker "relationships"—even when we appear to have more of them. Having more relationships also makes it appear that we are far more networked than we actually are. In reality, the truth is that most of us rarely take the time or make the effort to connect on a deeper, more human level with the new people we meet. Yet, relationships have always needed that personal component to grow. Without the personal touch, and in today's world, it's all too easy to let dozens of potential contacts, friends, and mentors slip by as we sit glued to our never-ending streams of texts and emails. Sure, technology can be used to keep a relationship thread strong, but without meaningful face-to-face contact that thread can disappear entirely.

I find this an interesting phenomenon since people are still people who still want to work with those they consider friends. The only way to form that kind of bond, and to do it quickly, is to know the person we're meeting—not just as a business contact, but as an individual. I encourage this kind of attention to detail with my whole team. We're a lean operation, one in which everyone contributes, not only in our given roles, but to our business development as a whole. We manage these connections through introductions to friends and former colleagues, by meeting new people at conferences and other events, and through other venues.

Just as individual success relies on the strength of your network, an organization's success often hinges on the cumulative effect of combining the networks you and your colleagues bring to the table. Even a team that's working well, and efficiently, isn't maximizing its potential if the different teammates aren't aware of how to develop their spheres of influence. What do you need? A truly "networked organization," where each teammate is dedicated not only to expanding, but strengthening their professional relationships.

This is where Molly Wendell comes into the picture. Molly's years of experience working for and with corporate teams, finding executive talent for organizations, and consulting as a networking expert and speaker places her at the heart of developing what she has coined The Networked Organization®. Her innate ability, honed to perfection, of meeting new people and making them friends and clients in the blink of an eye is legendary. It is also a skill we can all learn if we put our hearts into following the techniques so ingeniously laid out in this book.

But where Molly's advice really packs a punch is in its directness and its ability to encourage us to take a chance—to see opportunities in places and at times when we may not have in the past. Molly invites us to go beyond the idea of simply finding new contacts by asking us to put ourselves out there in a way that makes others excited about building relationships with us, an approach that leads to opportunity. After spending 20 years in the technology industry, Molly is someone who knows firsthand that for all our technological advances that help us "connect," it's still the personal contact that matters most.

Join Molly in The Networked Organization and the many others who know that the key to success is relationships, and that, while forming relationships might start with one person, the bonds of those relationships will travel all the way through, and affect every level of, the entire organization.

So what now?

Read Molly's book with an open mind. Ask yourself how you can apply her concepts. Make the commitment to apply them with your team, division, or company. Start today.

As Molly says, "Every day that passes by, your organization is missing out the opportunity for better collaboration, the opportunity for greater performance, the opportunity for real revenue—the opportunity to truly become The Networked Organization."

INTRODUCTION

I hear comments like these all the time. This leads me to believe that the idea of networking is extremely unappealing to many people. Maybe even to most people. But it doesn't have to be.

For whatever reason, networking has gotten a bad rap. People who are not fans of it think it's purely superficial. Those who are good at it know otherwise. They know that it goes much deeper than that. They know that the tactical nature of networking offers you the ability to strategically form the bonds of real, meaningful relationships. They know that meaningful relationships don't occur overnight. They take time and attention to form and cultivate.

While building relationships can be harder than we'd like to think, it can also be easier than we think. It all depends on your motivation and what you want to get out of the effort you make. Sometimes it's about working better with the team; sometimes it's about finding a new team with which to work. Maybe your organization is trying to build its business, or get a referral to the right service provider. Maybe you simply want to make new friends. Any way you look at it, building relationships takes time. It takes energy. Quite simply, it takes work.

Work that is easier for some than it is for others.

Molly, it's easy for you, people often tell me. *You're a natural at this.* The reality is, it *is* easy for me. But only because I've been practicing since I was four years old. That's right. Four! As the youngest of five, while all of my siblings were off in school every day, I was home. And while I loved spending so much time with my mother as she ironed clothes and sang from the seemingly never-ending greatest hits collections of Petula Clark and The Lettermen, I needed a little more.

One day, I simply turned to my mother and said *Mom, I'm going visiting.* And off I went.

Our suburban Detroit neighborhood was a mix of young families and senior citizens, but it was the senior citizens who were available to visit during school hours. I can't imagine how it must've looked: little me, knee-high to a grasshopper, at their door announcing *Hello, I've come to visit.*

One thing I learned very quickly was that senior citizens liked to talk about their lives, and about life in general. I also learned that, just like me, they liked candy.

I quickly sorted our elderly neighbors into categories, depending upon their offerings. The Lewises, our next-door neighbors, were big fans of white chocolate. Mrs. Mills, down the street, served tea in a delicate tea service that made me feel as if I were visiting with the Queen of England. She also had toffee—which I loved—and was a natural networker, always interesting to me because she was interested *in* me. She asked about my family and looked for ways to help people (today I'd call it "providing value"). For example, Bill, Mrs. Mills' next-door neighbor, had cherry trees, and Mrs. Mills arranged it so my siblings and I could pick fresh cherries.

At the end of the block were the Blackstocks. The Blackstocks had a collie named Molly, which was nice, but more importantly, they had cookies. Every so often I'd check to see if the Reddies were home, too. Although they weren't home very often, I loved to skip up to their door just for the experience because it was like the entrance to a castle. The Reddies also gave out the best candy at Halloween!

Sometimes I'd make my last stop at Mrs. Ralston's house. Mrs. Ralston had a son a couple years younger than I, but he napped a lot.

By the time I was ready to start school myself, I had already built a network of neighborhood allies—all of whom held more authority and commanded more respect than any four-year-old could.

So, I guess I'd have to say that my life as a natural networker all started in pursuit of candy and company at the ripe old age of four. And when you practice something from such a tender age, you're bound to end up pretty good at it.

Soon after graduating from college, I learned another valuable lesson. I was working for IBM Corporation and traveling often for work. Because I traveled so much, I found myself with the opportunity for upgrades to first class. Whenever I was upgraded to first class, I felt compelled to make conversation with the person sitting next to me, usually a middle-aged corporate type and almost always an executive. My compulsion was driven by the fact that I never wanted anyone to think *Oh, I got stuck next to her.* I wanted them to walk away saying *Wow, how lucky was I that she was seated next to me.*

On one particular flight, I turned to the man next to me and asked what he did. Turns out he was the president of a pharmaceutical business. I had just finished reading the book *Strong Medicine*, a novel about the pharmaceutical industry by Arthur Hailey, so I had lots of good questions about the pharma business, clinical trials, FDA approval, and the like. About 20 minutes into the conversation—which consisted of me asking questions and him answering them—he looked at me. *What pharmaceutical company do you work for?* When I told him that I worked for IBM, he shook his head. *Molly, you know more about our business than my own people. If you ever want a job in this business, you let me know.*

You know what I was thinking? I was thinking, maybe your people should read *Strong Medicine*. Then they'll know just as much about pharma as I do.

Somewhere along the way, I realized that the way I got people talking was by asking smart questions about their business. This insight led me to read every book that Arthur Hailey wrote: *Wheels*, about the auto industry, *Hotel*, about the hospitality industry, *The Evening News*, about the broadcast business and *Airport*—well, maybe I saw the movie on that one. When I ran out of those, I read *Fortune Magazine* cover to cover. I figured that if I could learn enough about every industry, I would know the right questions to ask to keep just about any conversation going. And I was right. In fact, most people I met assumed I was part of their industry solely based on my questions.

It's still like that today. When I meet a lawyer, she thinks I'm a lawyer. When I meet a doctor, he thinks I'm a doctor, too. When I meet people in healthcare, they assume I'm in healthcare. Even the wind energy consultant I met thought I was in wind energy.

I try to stay up on trends in particular industries. I try to keep abreast of who's doing what. I try to know enough to ask the right questions to start the conversation.

In the book *Outliers*, Malcolm Gladwell talks about the concept of the 10,000-Hour Rule. He says the key to success in any field is a matter of practicing it for 10,000 hours. So, from the age of four up to my current age of something like 29 (that's right, again), yes, I've been practicing networking for more than 10,000 hours. But here's a hot tip. You don't need to spend 10,000 hours practicing networking to gain mastery of it. If you follow this book, you'll be able to master it more quickly. Much more quickly.

Let's say you're somewhere beyond the age of four, though, and feel as if you're behind the eight ball. What's important to remember is that it's never too late to start. The opportunity to have a conversation is always right around the corner. And the opportunity to become highly skilled at building relationships is closer than you think.

Now, turn the page and get one step closer to The Networked Organization®.

THE NETWORKED ORGANIZATION

1.1

NETWORKING
IS NOT A DIRTY WORD

Does the concept of *networking* make you cringe? Cause you to run the other direction? If it does, you're not alone.

Somewhere along the way, the world assigned a negative connotation to the word. So much so that many of us simply refuse to use it, call it something less threatening like "building relationships," or avoid the idea altogether. We find this description of relationship building much more acceptable. It's easy to see why, since all of us have spent our entire lives building relationships of one sort or another…with family members, friends, and colleagues. So why, you might ask, when it comes to the idea of networking for the express purpose of *building relationships*, do we find people go out of their way to avoid it altogether?

> Networking asks you to be
> ## GENUINE,
> ## AUTHENTIC,
> ### AND CURIOUS
> —to listen rather than talk.
> Have positive intent. Find the fascinating.

It might be because many people are uncomfortable with the idea of talking about themselves. It might be because many people think that networking is just another form of "schmoozing."

Here's the naked truth. Schmoozing is actually very different from networking. Schmoozing by its very nature implies you're superficial, disingenuous, and focused on yourself. Networking asks you to be genuine, authentic, and curious—to listen rather than talk. To have positive intent toward others and find the fascinating about them. Not to "show up and throw up."

Authentic networking is all about focusing on the other person, not yourself. Focusing not on the potential value to you alone, but the value to the greater network. Focusing on and embracing the idea of networking as a strategy with benefits, so that you can begin to see the power and potential in *all* your relationships.

I first talked about how to network and why it's so important in my book *The New Job Search*. I was sick and tired of people hanging out online, getting sad, lonely, and depressed when they didn't get any response from the internet black hole. *Get out and network!* I told them over and over. *But this time, do it right. Don't just tell everyone your life story. Learn about theirs instead. Be interesting by being interested.*

Those who listened to this advice found my strategy actually worked. They found themselves feeling more comfortable about picking up the phone and calling people, asking for a meeting, working the room at networking events. In essence, they were more comfortable with the very idea of getting out there and networking. More and more people who read my book were getting interviews and nailing those interviews and then landing coveted positions. Most importantly, instead of being sad, lonely, and depressed, they were actually enjoying the experience of the job search process.

It didn't take long before these same people began to think beyond the job search. *Molly, I've landed a job. Now what? How do I keep up my networking? What should I do to continue to build relationships? How can I take this newfound (or refined) networking skill and develop it even further?*

Answering these kinds of questions is what led me to write *The Networked Organization*. Because the importance of networking doesn't end when you land a job. In fact, when you're working, the importance of networking becomes that much greater.

1.1

The Networked Organization

Networked Organizations are comprised of people who truly value relationships. People who value their internal relationships with fellow co-workers and intentionally seek to increase collaboration. People who value their external relationships and intentionally seek to identify additional opportunity for the organization.

Given that you are reading this book, you are probably on board with the idea that building relationships is important. Perhaps you want to make it just a little easier for yourself and your team. My hope? That you are also on board with the idea that *you* can make a major difference in the success of your organization.

You have an incredible opportunity to be an integral part of the Networked Organization. Because the Networked Organization doesn't start with the organization itself. It starts with the people who ARE the organization. It starts with *you*.

This book is much more than a reference guide to networking. Sure, it has plenty of hands-on practical tips and new approaches that you can use immediately. Its true value, however, is more strategic because it shows you how to create a culture of networking within your organization.

It has become very clear to me over time that companies that embrace and practice the art and science of networking throughout the organization—not just in their sales force—are better positioned to thrive in both up markets and down ones. Companies that not only embrace but build a culture of networking are more likely to withstand market challenges and competitive pressures, and will attract the best talent.

1.1

Who wouldn't want to be a part of that?

How this book is organized

Section I, The Networked Organization, defines how a Networked Organization creates value and introduces the 7 Hard-and-Fast Rules of successful networking.

Section II, Building Networked Relationships, helps you define your desired network and navigate social media tools to support it.

Section III, Real World Networking, focuses on the tactical and practical elements relative to networking events and other networking opportunities that continually present themselves, whether on airplanes, at dinners, or at football games.

Real World Networking also discusses how to successfully get and leverage referrals.

Section IV, The Relationship Process, talks about orchestrating meetings: how to get them, what to do when you're there, and how to avoid wasting time. In Smart Networking Questions—my favorite section—I spend some time on developing smart questions. This section also includes suggestions for sound networking etiquette where, in our current environment, manners tend to walk out when technology walks in.

Finally, Section V, Maximizing Networked Relationships, discusses networking behaviors that support your greatest chance for success.

How to best put this book to use

Some of you will read this book and file it away on a shelf somewhere. Its real power, however, is in its ongoing use as a tool—a guide for both individuals as well as organizational leadership.

1.1

For the individual

The Networked Organization provides guidance through concrete examples and a simple set of rules on effective networking and building fruitful relationships. Generally, my readers say they like to tab, highlight, and reference the parts that speak to them the most so that the practices become a natural part of their life. Not sure what kind of people you want in your network? Look at your tabbed Section 2.1. Don't remember what you need to know as you're headed to your next networking event? Hustle to Section 3.2. You've secured a meeting, now what? Check out Section 4.2.

For the senior executive

The Networked Organization provokes new ways of thinking about the value and intent of networking within the company.

What if everyone in the organization worked together more seamlessly? What if they built relationships and identified even just one additional opportunity per year? Instead of relying solely upon the sales team to generate opportunities, what if you had dozens, hundreds, maybe even thousands of incremental opportunities to grow the business? This cultural shift could have a profound impact on the results of the organization.

27

If these are the kinds of questions you ask yourself after reading *The Networked Organization*, then I've done my job to open your eyes to a virtually untapped resource for becoming more effective and growing your business. These resources and tools are not meant to turn everyone in your organization into a salesperson, but to allow you and your team to identify and tap into that vast world of opportunities quite possibly right at your fingertips.

How to implement The Networked Organization

For most organizations, the ideas presented here represent a major shift in organizational culture and thinking. Clearly, there are a number of possible ways to initiate the goal of moving into a more intentional relationship building culture. It could start with having employees read this book, or be as extensive as creating and deploying an ongoing training program with supporting communication.

Organizational change projects can take the form of cascaded communications, starting with a meeting of C-suite executives who engage their direct reports, who then take the message to their teams, who lead local meetings with individual contributors: in other words, a consistent and cadenced program over a period of time.

Deployment might occur through a series of webinars and training classes for all employees. Some companies initiate change projects by holding discussions on a different topic from *The Networked Organization* each week. The key is to put the learning in context through employee engagement to gain their buy-in and ownership of the process.

An extensive global survey and study by IBM about how to make change work has demonstrated that leadership involvement, employee engagement, and honest communication are prerequisites for successful change. Creating and reinforcing a Networked Organization is by no means a simple task. And regardless of the approach to implementation your company takes, the key is to start at the top and reinforce behavior throughout. Talk the talk. Walk the walk.

What better way to connect top management with more people throughout your organization than a perfectly orchestrated culture of networking?

What better way to help your employees feel they're not only part of the process, but the most critical component, than by giving each and every one the power to make an incredible impact on the organization?

Hopefully, organizations will embrace and train their people in the concepts presented here. Hopefully, your teams will dedicate themselves to putting these concepts into practice. There's so much that teams can do to work better together. There's so much that we all can do to identify and leverage opportunities available to the organization. There's so much benefit that is ready to be realized.

The underlying theme of The Networked Organization is a simple one. What I talk about in the forthcoming pages isn't complex, and some of the tactics you probably already employ. What I've tried to do, though, is be very straightforward, help you understand the effects of your actions—which may or may not be what you intended—and organize the content in a way that makes it easy for you to put it into practice.

The bottom line? Teams who embrace the concepts in *The Networked Organization* will see not only increased collaboration, performance, and revenue, but will have more fun along the way.

It's a bold idea for those bold enough to embrace it.

1.1

NETWORKED ORGANIZATIONS CREATE VALUE

Networked Organizations create value by focusing on building relationships.

Someday, some way, you're going to need something from someone. And that something might not even be for you. It might be a favor for a friend, a neighbor, a co-worker, or someone's son or daughter. The more you focus on building relationships, and the more real relationships you have based on that focus, the easier you'll find it to get things done. Are you ready for that someday?

Most people think networking is only important for salespeople and job seekers. I'm here to tell you the ability to build relationships is a lifelong skill that helps you succeed in anything you do. It also helps make you indispensable.

In Networked Organizations everyone becomes indispensable.

I was talking to Jeff Pizzino, my public relations guy. I couldn't understand why it was so difficult to get me on the news in New York. Pay no mind that it's the number one TV market in the United States. Jeff is good at what he does. In fact, he's one of the best PR people I've ever met, and I've met a lot of them. As I sat there strategizing with him, I wondered aloud, *Jeff, why do people hire one salesperson over another?* Sensing the rhetorical nature of my question, Jeff hesitated. *Because they're better at selling?*

Sure, that's one answer. They have to be good at selling, but assuming you have a degree of competence in selling skills, what's the one thing that will set you apart from every other candidate?

Who you know. Your network.

That's when it struck me. Having the skill set for your functional area is really just the bar for entry. It's your network that makes or breaks you. I looked at Jeff. *Here's what I think*, I told him. *You're good. Really good. But to be really great, you need to get a better network. Instead of trying to pitch the media, you need the ability to make one or two phone calls, get connected with the right person, and then use your PR pitch skills to perfection to get me on TV in New York.* Two weeks later, I was featured on television in New York City.

I started thinking about the other professionals I deal with. Recently, we had an issue where a hotel overcharged us. The bill had come to me for resolution. I realized how much I would have preferred—and appreciated—if my financial accounting firm had settled the issue without my involvement. But to do that, it would have had to have an already established relationship with the hotel. An established relationship would have enabled them to deal with the situation and simply let me know when it had been successfully resolved. An established relationship would mean that if we had a really big problem, I could fully expect them to call the corporate office of the hotel chain and talk with their contacts in finance. Now *that* would be valuable. *That* would set them apart from every other accounting firm.

What makes *you* valuable? Your work ethic? Your competence? Your experience? Sure. But what makes you indispensable? *Your relationships.*

Your relationships give you the ability to get a meeting, get a resolution, get a credit, get a favor…with just one phone call. That saves you time, and the company money.

I met with a lawyer recently. Unlike most attorneys I know, this one said, *We can do the transactional work for you just like any other law firm. But my goal is to add value to your business. I want to help you with strategy. I know a lot of people who could provide incredible resources to you; resources in the form of influencers, customers, investors, and advisors. I want to help you identify new businesses that set you up for incredible success.* Who wouldn't want this person aligned with their business?

You might be thinking, *I'm not generally in a role that is customer-oriented.* It is a common misconception that the only people who should leverage outside relationships are your sales team. Keep in mind that *every* role is customer-oriented because without customers, who needs employees, right?

Are you in information technology? Build relationships with the vendor of the products you support along with other customers who are running those applications.

Are you in human resources? Maybe you belong to the HR Association, but how much are you networking in circles other than those where your peers hang out? Try heading to some other functional associations, such as those for finance or sales or marketing. Venture to some industry associations that are similar to the operational aspects of your industry.

1.2

Are you in supply chain? You know what would make you really valuable? Understanding how other industries manage their supply chain. Understanding the cutting edge technologies they're using. And I'm not just talking about reading up on them. I mean actually building relationships with professionals in those industries. They're going to tell you things that

> Obviously, you can't know
> EVERYONE,
> but certainly you can know
> SOMEONE.

you'll never read in a book or article that can help you figure out how to bypass the iterative steps to achieve true transformational change in the way your supply chain operates. Then, when you run into a problem at your own company, you'll know who to call. Obviously you can't know everyone, but certainly you can know someone.

I could go on and on with every functional area. I won't. All I'll say is, you think you know enough people? You don't. You think you're well connected in your area of expertise? Think about the other relationships you need to build. Who are your customer's customers? Who are your customer's suppliers? Who are your customer's service providers? How do you build relationships with them to bring more value to the table?

You want to be truly indispensable? Build a better network.

Do you work for a Networked Organization?

Organizations, in particular, probably stand to benefit the most when all their employees are ingrained with the concept of building relationships. Can you imagine how much more a company could grow if everyone was focused on building relationships that would provide new opportunity to the company?

1.2

Have you ever been laid off, downsized, or otherwise no longer needed in an organization? Want to never be in that position again? Listen up.

A few years back, I boarded the plane, took my aisle seat, and struck up a conversation with the person at the window seat, Jim. No one was sitting in the middle at the time. In the short time we were on board, we had already started a fascinating conversation. So fascinating, in fact, that when the person who had the middle seat showed up, I scooted over and gave up my coveted aisle seat. I asked Jim how many people were at his company. He said *2,000*. I asked him how many people at his company were responsible for revenue generation. He thought about it for a minute and said *About 200*. Then I rephrased the question and asked him how many people at his company *should be* responsible for revenue generation. Jim smiled. *Two thousand, I guess.*

Yes. All 2,000. Every single person in the company should be contributing to the success of the company. Can you imagine if every single person was focused on creating one new referral for the company per year? That's potentially 2,000 new customers. And what if even half of the company built relationships with one potential prospect? That would still be 1,000 new prospective customers. With that many new prospects, you're bound to realize additional revenue and profit. What happens when your

1.2

QUESTION: How many people in your company should be responsible for revenue generation?

Why? Everyone Wins!

More profit

More promotions

Higher incomes

Better returns

10%

Not enough employees are revenue generators

100%

100% of employees are revenue generators

ANSWER: **Everyone**

company grows in revenue and profit? It has more opportunity. The opportunity to hire people. The opportunity to promote people. The opportunity to pay people more. The opportunity to provide better returns to your shareholders.

And who wins when everyone is focused on bringing in new customers?

Everyone. Everyone wins.

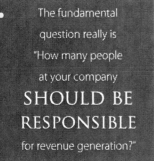

The fundamental question really is "How many people at your company SHOULD BE RESPONSIBLE for revenue generation?"

What happens when fewer people are focused on bringing in new customers? That's right, less opportunity. Fewer customers means hiring freezes, pay freezes, job cuts, and disenchanted shareholders. And who loses when everyone takes the attitude of *That's not my responsibility?*

That's right. Everyone. Everyone loses.

The fundamental question really is "How many people at your company should be responsible for revenue generation?" The answer? Everyone. Everyone at the company *should be* responsible for revenue generation, and therefore be building, maintaining, and leveraging relationships. Companies that think salespeople are the only ones who should be focused on producing new customers are completely missing the boat. Let me give you an example.

Tammy works in accounts payable for a software company selling security solutions to the heads of technology departments. When Tammy walks out the door of her office on Friday, how busy will she be? If she's like most people, pretty busy. But how much of her weekend will be spent thinking about the company? How often will she think about potential new relationships for the company as she gets ready for the dinner party she'll go to with her husband? When Tammy is at the party grabbing a few hors d'oeuvres and starts talking to Joe who works in technology for a potential customer, does Tammy make the connection? Does she continue the conversation, eventually suggesting she'd love to follow up with Joe next week to have him take a look at her company's solution and perhaps get his opinion and insight as to whether they have something unique and how they could make it better?

1.2

No, the typical Tammy simply grabs another bacon-wrapped shrimp and heads back to her husband's side, where she'll spend the rest of the night hamstringing them both from forging new and better relationships.

The next day, Tammy takes her 10-year-old daughter to her soccer game and sits on the sidelines for about an hour. She exchanges pleasantries with the other parents. One of them happens to work in finance for a potential customer. But does Tammy know that? No, because she doesn't spend any time getting to know them. She's too busy texting.

About two hours later, Tammy is off to her son's football game. Does she make conversation with the people next to, in front of, or behind her in the stands? No. No, she doesn't. Little does Tammy realize that she's again missing out on an opportunity. The general counsel for a major company in town, whose office happens to be two doors down from the technology decision maker, is sitting right in front of her.

After the football game, Tammy stops by the dry cleaners to pick up her clothes. There's a long line. Instead of thinking about how people who get clothes dry cleaned tend to work for a living where they get dressed up in dry-clean-only garments, Tammy makes a call to her sister. You know, the one she already knows. Tammy doesn't even realize she's standing in between two heads of human resources for major companies in town.

Later that evening, Tammy and her husband attend a fundraiser for their children's school. They're seated at a table full of other parents, but they spend most of the time talking to each other, because to them this is Date Night. They don't even think that the eight other people at the table may be great opportunities for relationships. What could have really been useful was to talk to Ben, seated two chairs away from Tammy. Turns out that Ben runs admissions for the university that her son is interested in attending. And that woman across the table runs finance for a growing company and is looking for someone to head her accounts payable team. Who knows? Maybe they could've been really good contacts.

Sunday comes along, and Tammy and her crew head off to church. They get there just as the service is about to begin. There's coffee and doughnuts after the service, but instead they make a beeline for the parking lot.

In one weekend, Tammy has come across opportunities to build relationships with no fewer than 10 people—and probably a lot more. But how many relationships—outside of the ones she already had—has she fostered? None. That's right. Zero! And here's the crazy part. This is what her schedule is like almost every weekend.

Monday morning Tammy is back at work where she learns that the company is going through some struggles and they need to reduce the company workforce by 10%. Tammy is let go. *What could I have done differently*, she wonders?

Hmm…I know, Tammy. I know what you could've done differently. In addition to doing your job, you could have provided so much additional value to the company that when it came time to reduce

1.2

Potential professional relationships are all around you.

Don't waste opportunities to make connections.

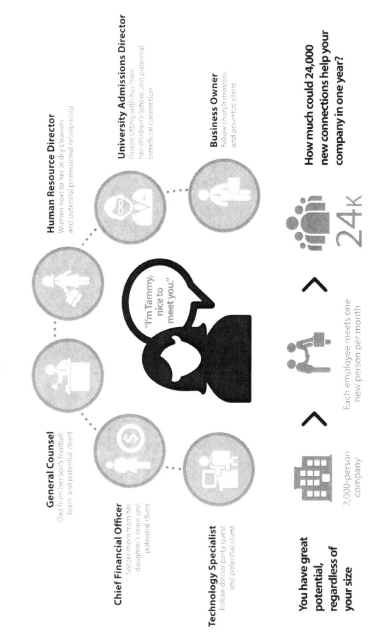

Chief Financial Officer
Soccer mom from her
daughter's team and
potential client

General Counsel
Dad from her son's football
team and potential client

Human Resource Director
Woman next to her at dry cleaners
and potential professional relationship

University Admissions Director
Parent sitting with her from
her children's school and potential
beneficial connection

Technology Specialist
Fellow dinner party guest
and potential client

Business Owner
Fellow church member
and potential client

"I'm Tammy,
nice to
meet you."

**You have great
potential,
regardless of
your size**

2,000-person
company

> Each employee meets one
new person per month

> 24K

**How much could 24,000
new connections help your
company in one year?**

the workforce, your name would never have been on that list. And even if it were, you would already have had the network you needed for future opportunities in place.

Most people have the opportunity to meet at least 10 new people each and every week. But do they? No. In fact, most people outside your sales organization don't meet one person per month, let alone per week. What would happen if you focused on meeting one new person per month? That's 12 new people a year. A great start! What if everyone at your company had the same goal to meet one new person each month? At a 2,000-person company, that's 24,000 people. Even if we're conservative and reduce that number by half, that's still 12,000 people. Could 12,000 new relationships benefit your company? Maybe.

> Most of the time, it's not even about getting out there more; it's about
>
> # LEVERAGING
>
> what you have when you're already out there.

Or perhaps you work for a small firm of just 50 people. Using the same formula, your team could meet up to 600 people per year. Could 600 new relationships benefit your company? Heck, could 10 new relationships benefit your company? Probably!

It's possible that these new contacts are not all necessarily in a position to buy from your company, but they are certainly in a position to open up their network to you should they choose. What are you doing to foster those relationships and give each person a desire to help you or refer you or your company?

Most of the time, it's not even about getting out there more, because most people are out there in some form or fashion week in and week out. It's about leveraging what you have when you're already out there.

When was the last time your head of finance, or marketing, or human resources, or manufacturing, or any department other than sales, for that matter, made an introduction to a potential new client? How many of your board members do this on a regular basis? It's not their job, right? Why not? Isn't the success of the company everyone's job? Isn't that the kind of people you want associated with your organization?

1.2

Next time you think about making hiring decisions, or even firing decisions, you might consider thinking about the Tammys and everyone else in your office. Who do you want in your organization? Perhaps someone who takes so much pride in your company that they think about providing benefit even while they're not on the clock.

Maybe you, as an employee, are just like Tammy. What do you owe your company? You give them an honest day's work and they pay you in return. Isn't that enough? Well, not really. Maybe you owe your company a little more than you think.

You see, I have a passion not only for loyalty, but for commitment, which I believe is a two-way street. Does this mean that because a company pays you a fair wage, your obligation is to give fair work back? No. I believe that when a company employs you, the compensation and benefit package is only part of the equation. The majority of benefit for you is that the company is providing not only an identity, but a level of security and a purpose in life.

As much as we'd like to think that our work does not frame our identity, the harsh reality is, it does. While some might like to think that our jobs don't define us, that they're not our identity, the truth clearly says otherwise.

Ask anyone who's been out of work for more than six months. Ask them where their identity went. Let's face it, without a paying job, most of us who rely upon an income are pretty insecure about who we are.

The company that pays you is providing you with an identity by removing a level of insecurity that only the state of joblessness creates. What can you do to reciprocate? That's easy. You can become an active participant in helping your organization become a *Networked Organization.*

Don't you want to see your company grow and prosper? Don't you want to be a part of that growth? If you could do something about it, wouldn't you want to? Because if you don't, there are plenty of other people out there who would love to have your job and give back to the organization!

I can't get the thought out of my head that people in organizations everywhere have the ability to make a difference to the bottom line every month, every week, every day. And don't. It not only makes me mad; it makes me sad. I don't think they intentionally don't do it. The problem is that they don't intentionally *do* it. They have no intention around it, and therefore, don't even think about it. But what if everyone at your company had intention around it? What if everyone at your company made an effort? What progress would your company realize?

The culture of a Networked Organization

Creating a Networked Organization is more than creating a culture of pride. It's creating a culture of ultimate teamwork. A culture of being all-in-this-together. A culture where each and every person shares in the success of the organization and knows that she or he can do one more thing to make a difference. A culture of *networking*.

1.2

Honestly, I don't know too many organizations that have this kind of culture. In the past 20 years, so many companies have had layoffs and downsizings. The people who leave have a bitter taste for the organization; those who remain have double and triple the work—and have to do it with the looming thought that they might be next. It's tough to maintain, let alone grow, an organization when everyone has one foot out the door.

Networking isn't only for outside the organization

But this isn't only about networking outside your organization. It's also about building relationships inside your organization. It used to be that you went to an office where you connected with your co-workers, had coffee, had lunch. But now, our world is becoming a placeless society. Geographically neutral. Many firms—large, medium, and small—are figuring out how to enable employees to work virtually. You might go days, weeks, and even months without being face-to-face with many of your co-workers. Your networks are limited to those you already know and those with whom you need to interact in order to get your job done today.

Though work is becoming more and more distributed, networks are not. While more work is piling on, people are looking for innovative ways of doing more with less. Here's where knowing the right people in the organization can help, people who know how and where to go to get things done. If you're not actively focused on building your network within the organization, you may never find these people. While you have your company in common, chances are you have little else. That is, until you build that network. And building it takes time.

Networking within

The same is true whether you're networking inside or outside the organization: the same techniques apply. More importantly, the same benefits apply. An effective network makes you a more productive employee. It makes your job easier by knowing the right people. It helps you earn your next promotion by being visible to the right people. It helps you when you're in a jam, helps you launch a new idea you've been thinking about for years, and helps you achieve greater success, both personally and professionally. An effective network is there for you for the rest of your life.

Networking for introverts and extroverts

But wait, you say. This idea of networking is easy for you, Molly. You're an extrovert.

> Where do you get your energy? From being **ALONE** or being surrounded by **OTHER PEOPLE?**

I hear this all the time. And the truth is that I *am* an extrovert—meaning that I get my energy from being around other people. But that doesn't make me a better networker. In fact, being an extrovert can often work against me.

Extroverts may be great at getting out the door, but introverts hold the key to building better relationships. In general, introverts—people who get their energy from being alone—tend to be better networkers than extroverts for a couple of reasons. First, extroverts tend to talk too much. It's hard to build relationships when you're the one doing all the talking. Second, introverts typically hate talking about themselves, so they have a tendency to listen more.

1.2

Both camps have advantages and disadvantages in terms of networking. If you're an extrovert, you have to work harder at letting others do the talking without interrupting. Need to talk? On your way home from the event, call a friend and talk at them all you want. If you're an introvert, you have to work harder by making the commitment to get out and meet people. Need alone time? When you get home, hole up and don't say a word for the next 24 hours.

I think about my friend John. John and I met while he was in the job search. John is engaging and extremely friendly; he always has a smile on his face. Everyone who meets John immediately likes him. Only when he attended a brain profiling session I hosted did I learn that John was about as introverted as you can get. He had everyone fooled. He told me that networking was actually really difficult for him. *I have to spend some time psyching myself up for it,* he said, *and I am always completely drained after attending an event or two.* I was surprised because at the event, no one, including me, had been the wiser.

You see, John understands the bigger picture. That relationships don't simply appear out of thin air. That he has to seek them out. He knows that to build the right relationships, he needs to get out and network. And network he does! John has built an incredible network, because he has ingrained in himself the culture of networking.

Introverted or extroverted, the same techniques apply.

It's time to create value.

Right now, make the commitment that you're going to focus on being indispensable to the organization. That you're going to focus on being intentional about building relationships and identifying opportunities. That you're going to focus on becoming an active participant in helping your organization become a Networked Organization.

1.2

I.3

Building a Networked Organization from the Inside Out

Changing the culture *in* the organization can dramatically change the effects *of* the organization. In order to have a truly Networked Organization, you need to develop a culture of collaboration: a culture of working together internally. And yes, what I mean by that is that you actually need to start *talking* to each other.

How important is collaboration in the organizations of today? I was speaking with a college professor who was writing a book about hiring practices. When we reached the subject of collaboration, she asked me what I thought it meant when a company said they were highly collaborative. My quick answer was, *Many say they're highly collaborative, but very few actually are.*

It all comes down to semantics. Collaboration just isn't what it used to be, and the way organizations implement the idea of collaboration is changing. Collaboration used to be considered more of a spirit—a practice that invited employees to get in the same room and brainstorm or work through problems real time and interactively. But now, more often than not, "collaboration" takes the form of an electronic tool where others can create, edit, comment, or criticize a specific project or program.

1.3

And now we have a problem. This electronic tool contains very little actual communication—in fact, less than 20%. This highly efficient collaborative tool doesn't take into account voice, inflection, tone, or body language. Imagine if you were working on a puzzle and 80% of the pieces were missing. How easy would it be for you to comprehend and envision what you were trying to put together? Even if you could figure it out, wouldn't it be a lot easier and faster if you had that missing 80% of the puzzle?

Sure, electronic tools help with tracking, version control, and knowing where documents are stored, but are they really making your teams more collaborative? Are the individuals on your teams really working together like teams? Are they working toward the same goal while interacting on a personal level? Does your team work in the spirit of "we're all in this together" as the basis for collaboration? Probably not.

Some companies are engaging with social business software. Success is based on user adoption, and user adoption is based on value. When companies install these systems, they need to think long and hard about the tools and value they bring to the individual.

What they really ought to be doing is looking at these social business software networks not as a strategy, but a tactic within an overall strategy. Focus first on how you can bring people together and help them build relationships, and *then* utilize the tool to assist in maintaining and nurturing those relationships.

Life gets even more complicated when companies undergo mergers and acquisitions. Have you been part of one of those integrations lately—the one that looks so buttoned up on paper? If you have, you know how infinitely challenging they are in real life. Why? Because people are involved! Are your teams taking the time to build the relationships they need to come together as one team? Are they committed to a "we're all in this together" approach? Probably not.

Building relationships takes time, not technology.

We live in a world of online communication. What seemed like such a technological breakthrough is on the verge of creating a human breakdown. I love technology and embrace most of it, but when technology gets in the way of actually having a conversation, it's time to say enough is enough.

People have embraced technology because of its efficiencies. In the workplace, people email, instant message, and text all day long. Sound efficient? Absolutely. Is it effective? Not so much.

It reminds me of what Stephen Covey said in the *7 Habits of Highly Effective People*: "While you can think in terms of efficiency in dealing with time, a principle-centered person thinks in terms of effectiveness in dealing with people."

The technology default: efficiency versus effectiveness

Here's the problem. When you default to technology for interaction too quickly and too often, you'll typically find that the only time there's an actual conversation, complete with voice, inflection, tone, and body language, is when the interaction has escalated into conflict. If you haven't given the relationship the personal touch and the time and attention it needs and deserves on which to build a solid foundation, the likelihood of a conflict is a very real outcome. If you're lacking the most basic elements of a relationship, how can interactions based on a shaky foundation be pleasant? Now ask yourself this: If this is your employee culture—one that defaults to technology too quickly and too often—what are the relationships truly like? I'll tell you what they are like all too often. Toxic.

The good news is that this behavior is easily fixed, but it definitely takes discipline. Imagine responding to almost every email, instant message, and text with a phone call or an in-person conversation. Will it take some extra time? Sure. Will your co-workers think you're nuts? Probably. Will they get tired of you calling when you could've replied electronically? Perhaps. But here's what you're doing. You're secretly laying the groundwork for a real relationship, the kind of relationship that builds over time, the kind of relationship you'll

Sorry my email is
SO LONG.
I would have written a
SHORTER ONE,
but I didn't have the
TIME.

continue to have because you've invested so much time into it. Basically, the kind of relationships that we all had at work years ago. The kind of relationship that tends to last a long time…maybe even a lifetime.

Aren't you tired of conversations via email? Aren't you tired of the seven texts it takes to schedule one meeting? Aren't you tired of people thinking you're available 24/7?

Aren't you tired of all this communication where everyone expects you to respond in an instant without regard for your schedule, obligations, responsibilities or memory? *I'm sorry, your email got buried in the 200 other ones I received yesterday. Yes, I forgot you texted me. I guess if it was that important, you would have picked up the phone and called me.*

We aren't just talking about respect for someone else's schedule. We're talking about true effectiveness.

On NPR's *Talk of the Nation*, the hosts spoke about an interesting study that looked at the most effective means of communication in the workplace. What did the study find? All this texting, instant messaging, and emailing back and forth does nothing to improve effectiveness. Research shows that it takes two people up to nine times longer to accomplish a simple conversation using electronic means than if they simply speak on the phone or in person. If you add complexity into such a conversation, it takes much longer—and there's no guarantee that you will accomplish the result you were seeking. This probably doesn't surprise you.

What is surprising, however, is how so many people ignore these findings and continue to use text, email and instant messaging for even the most important and complex conversations.

Again, 80% of all communication is non-verbal (body language, tone, inflection), yet when you move to electronic means to communicate, you lose all of that. No matter how carefully crafted your email may be, more often than not, it will be completely misinterpreted by the recipient. And you'll likely never know.

Here's a test. Say these words in a voice that expresses concern over timing: *When are you going to get me that file I asked for?*

Now say the same words in a voice that reflects anger and frustration: *When are you going to get me that file I asked for?*

In the first example, I may simply want to know what time the file will arrive, maybe in the morning, maybe the afternoon. In the second example, I'm sending the message that you are at fault, you've messed up…and I've lost my patience.

Here's the underlying problem. Words can easily be misinterpreted. You can review and edit your emails all day long, but still, there's a very real chance that elements of it will be misunderstood. You can reduce this risk by talking directly with someone.

Most people write emails assuming a tone of positive intent; most people **READ EMAILS** assuming a tone of **NEGATIVE INTENT.**

It all comes down to trust. Interestingly, most people WRITE emails assuming a tone of positive intent. Yet, without a strong, trusted relationship, most people READ emails assuming a tone of negative intent.

If that reality doesn't make you want to pick up the phone and have a conversation, what will? But, don't worry. You don't need to change. Because nobody misinterprets *your* emails…right?

I've seen many an employee cop out by emailing when he really should have picked up the phone and had the conversation he needed to have. People think email is so efficient because you can "talk at" a lot of people in a short timeframe—without giving them a

1.3

chance to answer in the moment. But isn't it more effective to have an actual conversation where you can determine opportunities and gain closure?

You can keep texting. You can keep emailing. You can even instant message. But if you really want to build solid, successful relationships and have true collaboration, you need to learn to pick up the phone, or better yet, meet with people in person. Have real live conversations with real live people.

1.3

When does collaboration begin?

Optimally, collaboration should begin on day one of work. Managers need to build into their organizational budgets the cost of building internal relationships—the cost of true collaboration; of networking within. How many organizations are putting onboarding programs in place for their new employees? Training programs are a thing of the past. What used to be six-to-eight-month training programs are now six-to-eight days, and sometimes just six-to-eight minutes. Organizations expect new employees to hit the ground running. They'll hit the ground all right, but it won't be running.

Most organizations are not setting their new employees up for success. It's probably not intentional, but at the end of the day, the result is the same. They're swimming or sinking on their own.

How difficult would it be to make sure every new employee has networking meetings with five other employees per day for the first week. I've seen organizations take a back seat approach to this and tell new employees to schedule the meetings themselves. How do the new employees even know with whom to meet? It would be better if human resources or the reporting manager scheduled these for the employee and had them in place already. That would be a good start. Imagine meeting 25 other associates, learning

When should collaboration begin?

Collaboration should begin on Day One of work.

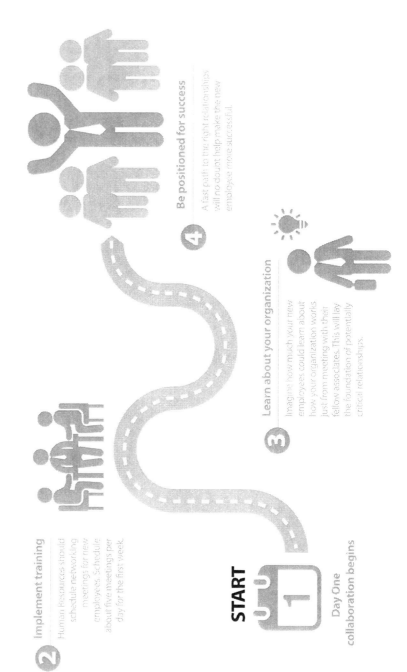

START

1

Day One
collaboration begins

2 Implement training

Human Resources should schedule networking meetings for new employees. Schedule about five meetings per day for the first week.

3 Learn about your organization

Imagine how much your new employees could learn about how your organization works just from meeting with their fellow associates. This will lay the foundation of potentially critical relationships.

4 Be positioned for success

A fast path to the right relationships will no doubt help make the new employee more successful.

what they do, building the foundation of a relationship. Imagine how much your new employees could learn about how your organization works. Imagine the fast path to the right relationships that will help make this new employee successful. Onboard that, people!

What about your current employees?

Employees used to be able to network with other employees at their organization's annual conference. Sadly, many organizations have gotten rid of annual conferences. But is the price they're paying for not having the conference greater than the price they would have paid to have it? Attendees don't participate in conferences solely for the content. They participate because they know that much of the insight will come from meeting other people and seeing what else is going on in the industry or company. Smart meeting planners build enough opportunity for networking, facilitated networking, into the program to benefit the attendees.

What about putting a relationship building program in place that encourages all employees to identify one person they don't know well, or at all, and start with a 30-minute get-to-know-you session? This doesn't have to be a daily program or even a weekly one. It doesn't have to be fancy. It doesn't have to cost a lot of money. It just has to be done. Managers could work with the employees to figure out with whom they should meet. Then, measure your results simply by debriefing each employee and your teammates on a monthly basis about whom they met and what they learned.

Sometimes you have to look outside your organization to network right back in. Don't be shy about looking at your network and seeing who knows whom at your company. That external referral may be exactly what you need to get some time on a busy executive's calendar.

The real value of what employees or team members learn may not surface until some time has passed, until he or she encounters an issue and needs something resolved. It's then that the value becomes very apparent.

Networking within helps you build a strong foundation for relationships. It helps you build trust. It helps you be more effective in your job. It helps you be a better steward of the organization. And, selfishly, it will likely help you get noticed for bigger and better opportunities within the organization.

Many companies reduce funding for internal conferences and meetings, then spend all kinds of dollars on programs and tools to increase collaboration. Where they err is in assuming that people will actually use these tools to collaborate. It's difficult to collaborate effectively without trust. It's even more difficult to have trust without the foundation of relationships.

Leveraging the value of your organization or ecosystem

One area where organizations continually fall short is leveraging their own resources.

I interact with a lot of venture capital (VC) and private equity (PE) firms. They invest in companies and obtain partial or full ownership. The group of companies in which they invest is called their portfolio. I've had many a conversation with these VC and PE firms about their portfolio, and how they are leveraging the companies to help each other.

Let's say a VC or PE firm had 30 companies in its portfolio. What if you segmented them by their target customer? And then held facilitated discussions with those teams to identify who knows whom, who's doing business with which targets, and then put a plan in place to leverage the relationships?

Many global organizations I know endeavor to do this as well—to leverage other divisions within the organization to identify additional business development opportunities—but it typically doesn't seem to pay off. I think the issue lies in the implementation. You can't just put people in a room and have them figure it out. It needs to be a coordinated and continued mindset and approach. It needs to be facilitated, documented, acted upon, and measured. And most importantly, it needs to be integrated into the business as a way of doing business.

These types of facilitated discussions hold great value. The organizations who do it right realize incredible, untapped opportunity, which shows up not only in their results but also in their employee satisfaction.

Devote the time to be truly collaborative.

Being truly collaborative takes time. It takes effort. It takes a bigger commitment than sending off an email and cc'ing 10 other people. But when you have collaboration, everything is easier. When you have trust, everything is easier. Set yourself and your employees up for success by creating an environment that encourages collaboration—not just through technology, but through real live interaction with real live human beings.

The Networked Organization Action Plan

- Pick up the phone! Next time you're about to send an email, pick up the phone and have a conversation instead.

- When you see an email that you read negatively, call that person for clarification.

- Set up meetings with five people from different departments with whom you don't normally interact.

- Onboard new employees with a personalized networking schedule. Include what each person does and potential areas of focus for the conversation.

I.3

The 7 Hard-and-Fast
RULES OF
Networking

Technique versus practice

Whether we are talking about internal or external collaboration and networking, there are rules that must be followed in order to be highly effective. Live by these rules. Practice implementing these rules. Remember, practice doesn't necessarily make perfect. More likely, practice makes permanent. So, my advice? Be careful what you practice.

Very few athletes do well in their respective sport without an intense focus on technique. They hire coaches to help with technique. World-class golfers, skiers, pitchers and swimmers will all tell you that technique makes all the difference. But you can't be great if all you have is technique. You also need to practice that technique.

Consider the basketball great Shaquille O'Neal. Shaq may have been incredible on defense, but was horrible at free throws. For every 10 free throws Shaq attempted, he was lucky to make five, going down in history as one of the worst free-throw shooters in the NBA. Free throws are supposed to be the easiest shots to make. It's just you and the basket. They don't call them free for nothing. How could someone at Shaq's level, someone so incredibly gifted in basketball, be such a horrible free-throw shooter? We know it's not because he didn't practice. Experts tell us that it's because he practiced with poor technique.

Without good technique, you risk injury, damage, or failure. That makes a lot of sense in sports. But what does it have to do with networking? Everything. Trust me. Severely damaged or failed relationships are a common result of the consistent practice of poor technique.

1.4

Setting the groundwork for networking technique

Perfecting your networking technique requires you to follow my hard-and-fast rules. During the course of this book, you'll be reminded how to apply and follow them. Some of you may think they are merely suggestions. They are not. Some of you will choose to use them at your leisure. Please don't. These rules are made never to be broken, and unless you embrace them—all of them—and practice them continually, your technique will always be subpar.

Molly's 7 Hard-and-Fast Rules of Networking

RULE 1 · · · · · · ▷ The Golden Rule: Networking is not about you

RULE 2 · · · · · · ▷ Build the well before you need the water

RULE 3 · · · · · · ▷ Be there and aware

RULE 4 · · · · · · ▷ Be interesting by being interested

RULE 5 · · · · · · ▷ Assume positive intent

RULE 6 · · · · · · ▷ Attitude is everything

RULE 7 · · · · · · ▷ Let them win

1.4

Molly's Networking Rule #1
(The Golden Rule)

Networking is not about you.

(See Section 3.1)

Believe it or not, networking is not about you. In fact, it's about everyone else but you. Much of what I talk about in this book is there to make the interaction more comfortable for the other person. Over time, you will start to see how the more comfortable you make it for others, the more comfortable and enjoyable it will be for you. But it always, always, starts with the other person.

The biggest secret—which is not really a secret at all since Dale Carnegie's been talking about the idea since the 1930s—is this: Get them to like you. When you talk to people, get them to talk about themselves. The more they talk about themselves, the more they like you. And the more they like you, the more they want to help you.

Molly's Networking Rule #2

Build the well before you need the water.

(See Section 2.1)

Don't just build the well. Define it. Identify the people with whom you want to establish relationships. Then, before you ask anything of them, figure out a way to provide value to them first.

Jay Allen, one of my business partners, calls this The Law of Two Favors. Always think about how you can help others and provide at least two favors before you ever call in a favor for yourself.

Too many people try to establish a relationship at the point in time when they need something from that other person. Too many people are keeping score. I gave you a favor, now you give me one. But life doesn't really work out that way. Those who keep score are focused on the wrong thing. Sometimes you give and give to certain people, only to receive from others. It's really true that what comes around, goes around; it's really true that the more you help others, the more help you will receive from others. What's important to recognize is that the help you give and the help you get doesn't necessarily come from the same people.

Start making a difference in the lives of others. In turn, you'll be amazed what a difference it will make in your own.

Molly's Networking Rule #3

Be there and aware.

(See Section 3.2)

Networking Rule #3 is one of the most difficult rules to follow. The world offers endless sources for distraction. Most of us are being pulled in so many different directions with too much to do and not enough time with which to do it. All you see these days is the top of people's heads because their faces are buried in their phones. They're either texting or talking or texting while talking. It seems no one is actually living in the moment. They're too busy recapping the past moments with someone they already know, or trying to figure out how to pack 10 hours of future moments into a five-hour time slot. I've been to countless events where people are so focused on when they're going to leave that I wonder why they ever bothered to show up.

If you want to perfect your networking technique, you need to get comfortable with the idea of being in the moment. Being present. Paying attention. Being aware of your surroundings. When you master those things, you won't have to pretend you're enjoying yourself. You *will* enjoy yourself.

Molly's Networking Rule #4
Be interesting by being interested.
(See Section 4.2)

1.4

One of the biggest secrets to relationship building is that the more interested you are in others, the more people find you interesting. Too often, people do what my friend Susan Ruhl describes as "show up and throw up." They show up at a networking event, a flight, or a meeting and begin talking. They continue talking and don't shut up until they've regurgitated their life stories onto anyone unfortunate enough to step into their path. No wonder so many people hate networking.

Good relationship builders, however, are genuinely curious. They're curious about others and their lives. They ask questions—thoughtful questions—because they are curious. They ask questions because they care. They continue asking questions because they want to know more. They know that the more you ask questions of others, the more interesting you yourself become. It's a strange but real phenomenon. Want to be more interesting? Be more interested.

Molly's Networking Rule #5

Assume positive intent.

(See Section 5.2)

Indra Nooyi, the first female CEO of Pepsi, said the best advice she ever received was from her father who told her to always assume the positive intent of others. In a *Fortune* magazine interview, Nooyi said that when you follow this advice, your whole approach becomes very different. You aren't defensive. You open your mind to really listening to what that person has to say. On the other hand, she went on to say, when you assume negative intent, you have a tendency to be defensive and angry. You're more likely to react emotionally.

This is really about trust. When you have strong, tested, trusting relationships, it's easy to assume positive intent. When you have weak, untested, and untrusting relationships, you might assume negative intent on the part of others. But, as we all know, trust is not that simple.

Typically when people join an organization they have a positive level of trust and are willing to extend that positive level until proven otherwise. Most people already part of the organization generally view this new person with a fairly neutral level of trust. Some, especially those who might have been candidates for the same position but didn't get it, view this new person with a negative level of trust. Either way, the mentality behind the common excuse for maintaining a neutral or negative level of trust takes the attitude: *You have to earn my trust first.*

Steven M. R. Covey, author of *The Speed of Trust*, talks about the behavior of trusted leaders. One of those behaviors incorporates the attitude of extending trust. You want to be trusted? Extend trust to others first. What if we changed our approach to view everyone as trustworthy until proven otherwise instead of the other way around? What if we regarded what others did with positive intent until proven otherwise? How much more effective could your organization be? How much more enjoyable could your organization be? How much more satisfied could your employees be?

Molly's Networking Rule #6

Attitude is everything.

(See Section 5.2)

It's your decision. You have a choice. Every day, you can choose to be positive or negative; to see people and things in a negative or positive light. You can choose how things will affect you. You can choose to be lifted up or let life drag you down. It's up to you. Remember when you were headed to your first day of kindergarten? Your mom let go of your hand and you joined the other kids headed for the classroom. Her parting words were *Make good choices!* Mom was right. It's in your power. You and you alone have the ability to choose how you will live your life. Sure, we all have bad things happen to us. But people who choose to be positive don't let those bad things define them. They understand that life has its share of ups and downs. Amazingly, people with positive attitudes tend to have more ups than downs.

Don't show up at work, at an event, in life, with a bad attitude. A happy person is far more attractive to others than a Negative Ned. If you're like Glum from *Gulliver's Travels*—always the pessimist—people won't like to be around you. If all you ever do is complain, pass on the bad news, and fuel the gossip, people will tire of listening. Quickly.

Be approachable. Be friendly. Walk around with a smile on your face. Greet others. Help others. Make it easy for people to be attracted to you.

My friend Michele O'Shaughnessy always says that a good measure of how approachable you are is how often strangers ask you for the time or directions. When was the last time someone asked you for directions? When was the last time you saw someone who needed help and, without being prompted, you reached out to lend a hand?

My husband did this in London. He met Bob, a senior executive for Shell Oil, on an airplane. Bob was meeting his wife at the theater, and because the flight was delayed, he might miss the opening of *War Horse*. After they deplaned, Tom went through the priority customs lane, and bought train tickets to the city—for both him and Bob. When Bob eventually got through, Tom was standing there with the train tickets. Bob made the show in the nick of time. Bob is now a friend for life!

Building relationships is much easier when you don't have to do all of the work. But first you need to make it easy for others to participate with you. Walk around with an attitude that makes you more approachable. Look for opportunities to lend a hand.

Molly's Networking Rule #7

Let them win.

(See Section 5.3)

This concept is so foreign to most people that I could write an entire book on the subject. What I'm talking about is practicing the art of refraining from one-upping people. When you one-up, you may think you're contributing to the conversation, but you're actually taking it away. Bit by bit. Piece by piece. You probably don't even realize you're doing it. Nobody ever tells you that you're not letting them win and they don't necessarily know how to express it. They begin to realize they don't like being around you because all you do is steal the conversation and make everything about you. Letting them "win" is not really about winning. It's about giving your turn to others because you understand that sometimes the greatest contribution you can make to a conversation is not making one at all.

> Sometimes the greatest **CONTRIBUTION** you can make to a **CONVERSATION** is not making one at all.

Here's how to go about it:

When friends tell you something that has them excited, let them have their day.

When co-workers tell you about a great accomplishment, let them have their glory.

When peers share a difficult situation with you, let them have their challenges.

Let someone else lose the most weight, buy the better house, get the better job, go on the greater vacation, have a child who is better/smarter/prettier than yours.

Let someone else be more tired, have the worse boss, survive the bigger vacation nightmare, deal with the flu that lasted longer. Who cares? You don't need to one-up them positively *or* negatively. Let them have their day—whatever kind of day they feel like having.

The Networked Organization Action Plan

- Copy this page twice.
- Put one copy of Molly's 7 Hard-and-Fast Rules of Networking by your desk—somewhere you can see it on a daily basis.
- Put the other copy in your wallet/purse to carry with you—and review it prior to going into a networking event or meeting.

Molly's 7 Hard-and-Fast Rules of Networking

RULE 1 — The Golden Rule: Networking is not about you

RULE 2 — Build the well before you need the water

RULE 3 — Be there and aware

RULE 4 — Be interesting by being interested

RULE 5 — Assume positive intent

RULE 6 — Attitude is everything

RULE 7 — Let them win

BUILDING NETWORKED
RELATIONSHIPS

THE INTENTIONAL NETWORK:
BUILDING YOUR
RELATIONSHIP PORTFOLIO

Realizing Molly's Networking Rule #2

Build the well before you need the water.

An *Intentional Network* is one that you consciously build. Over time, it essentially becomes a relationship portfolio—a diversified set of relationships that includes people from many different industries, geographies, and areas of expertise—similar to a financial portfolio that is comprised of diversified investments of stocks, bonds, and mutual funds. Strong relationships do not materialize overnight. They require dedication

I'm not your customer, BUT I KNOW YOUR CUSTOMER. And I know others who know your customer. Wouldn't you like to GET TO KNOW ME?

and conscious awareness. Remember this as you begin to create an Intentional Network. An Intentional Network is based on Molly's Networking Rule #2: Build the well before you need the water.

> Every few years, when my friend Tom needed something, he called Wally. Wally was gracious the first few times, but at one point he'd had enough. *You know,* he told Tom, *I'll help you, but don't wait another two years and then call me only because you need something again.*
>
> Wally's remarks really stung. Tom hadn't meant to be someone who always took and never gave. From then on, Tom made certain to be aware of his requests not only of Wally, but of everyone. He now goes out of his way to reach out to people, and Wally as well, to catch up, and offer up assistance even when he doesn't need anything.
>
> Especially when he doesn't need anything.

Tom's story isn't unusual. Typically, people reach out to you when they need something. Salespeople reach out to prospects when they want to sell something. Chief financial officers reach out to accounting vendors when they want to make a change. Most people only start thinking about *networking* when they need a job—which is unequivocally the worst time to reach out.

Does it feel as if most people only reach out to you when they need something? How often do you proactively reach out to help others?

Here's the thing: At no point in your life do you have worse leverage than when you need something from someone else. Don't get me wrong—there's nothing wrong with needing something from someone else—but the best time to reach out to people and nurture the relationship is when you don't need anything from them.

Are the relationships you've built

TODAY

the ones that will help you

SUCCEED

IN THE FUTURE?

One day, I was talking to Keith Ferrazzi, bestselling author of *Never Eat Alone* and *Who's Got Your Back*. Talking to Keith was enlightening. I consider myself pretty good at networking and more than above average when it comes to building and maintaining relationships. But something Keith said about my network being my net worth got me thinking. And thinking. And thinking.

The question that kept running through my mind was this: Are the relationships I've built today the ones that will help me succeed in the future? My answer? I didn't know. I really didn't know. Maybe they were. Maybe they weren't. The real truth was that I hadn't given it much thought.

I don't think I'm alone. I've lived my life helping people enhance their networks—to build new relationships. It's interesting. Virtually every person I've ever met is open to meeting someone who might be instrumental in their future success. I don't think there is ever the chance of running out of the possibilities for that to happen. But do people think about their network strategically? Do they make connections today with the chance they might need them tomorrow? Or is it more tactical, more from the perspective of *Hey, I have an issue right now. I wonder who can help?*

Everyone can use a hand, even the highest level executives who are typically insulated by their teams. I contacted an incredibly in-demand CEO of a thriving technology company to introduce her via email to someone I met on a plane because I felt there would be mutual benefit. By the next morning, I had an email from the CEO thanking me for the introduction along with her note to my airplane buddy. Yes, she was interested in talking. Yes, it looked like incredible opportunity for her company. Yes, she might be glad she made time for me when I reached out to her a few years ago and invited her to coffee.

But this is bigger than building the well before you need the water. This is about defining the well that you need to construct. And that's what I walked away with after talking to Keith, whose questions keep ringing in my ears over and over. Are the relationships I've built today the ones that will help me succeed in the future? Are the relationships all of your employees have—not just the ones your salespeople have—the ones that will help your organization succeed in the future? How are your current relationships helping or hindering you? Is it time to build some new relationships? Where do you begin?

We'll start with the *Who*.

Who do you want in your network?

This question sounds pretty overwhelming, but is probably the easiest to answer. Who you want in your network depends on what you're trying to accomplish. As my sixth-grade teacher used to tell me, *To be specific is terrific. To be vague is the plague.* This is just as true in networking. Without a specific plan around whom you're targeting, you may end up with an extensive network, but is it the network you want or need?

Competitive Forces

If you're looking to add value to your organization, and I truly hope you are, then one place to start could be with famed economist Michael Porter's model: The Five Forces That Shape Industry Competition.

The Five Forces That Shape Industry Competition

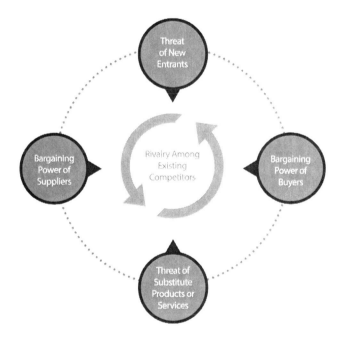

Porter's model suggests that companies compete for profits not just from direct competitors, but from other forces that shape the industry: the bargaining power of suppliers, the bargaining power of buyers/customers, the threat of new entrants to the marketplace, and the threat of substitute products or services—the alternatives to buying a product or service like yours. If you really want to be valuable to your organization, start with the Five Forces that Shape Industry Competition.

Begin by mapping out your direct competitors, suppliers, buyers, and substitutes. Write down the people you know in each area.

Start with buyers, target customers. When's the last time your team mapped out all of your contacts to determine who knows whom at your organization's target customers?

Segment these groups into size of organization. Meeting one person in a 10-person buyer organization may do the trick, but in a 2,000-person buyer organization, you'll want to build more than one relationship.

2.1

Figure out where the gaps are. Develop a plan to forge new relationships in those areas.

Identify people who provide complementary products or services to your customer. Think about what their network looks like.

The threat of new entrants is more difficult to discern. Sometimes you don't know they're going to be a competitor until they already are. Consider that and perhaps spend your time on those who are easier to identify.

Again, this exercise is not simply for the sales organization. It's for everyone in the company. The goal here is *intentional* relationship building.

Relationships Based on the Five Forces

Competitor	Supplier	Buyer/ Customer	Substitute/ Complementary Product & Service

2.1

Functional Area

Another way to look at your network is by functional area. Most people don't have deep relationships with others outside their own functional area. Most chief financial officers (CFOs) know other CFOs, but typically don't have a solid network of salespeople unless they're being sold to. Most supply chain managers don't have a solid network of marketing experts.

Start with the basic functional areas:

- General Management (Presidents/CEOs)
- Operations
- Finance
- Sales
- Marketing
- Human Resources
- Supply Chain
- Engineering
- Information Technology
- Legal

2.1

Set out to build a well-rounded functional network versus one that's skewed to a particular functional area.

Map out who you know. Fill in the gaps with who's missing.

1. Mark existing relationships with an X.
2. Mark desired relationships with an O.
3. Utilize those with an X, and others in your network, to get referred into those with an O.

Relationships by Functional Area

Name	Company	Date Met	GM	Ops	Fin	Sales	Mktg	HR	SC	Eng	IT	Legal
Irene Kinoshita	Ascolta	1990	X									
Jim Robinson	National Spine & Pain Centers	2008					X					
Wendy Ortiz	Walker Fine Prop.	1988				X						
Laurent Poirier	Hutchinson	2012								X		

2.1

Industry

Look at your network by industry. Does your network consist primarily of others in that same industry? If so, you might consider venturing out to begin to build relationships with people from other industries. Many people have backgrounds consisting of multiple industries, but what you need is a good cross-section of people in different industries today. People who know what the trends are, where the industry is going, what's relevant right now. Figure out how your industry is similar and different from theirs. Understand the key drivers to profitability, the competitive landscape, and which dynamics are changing the nature of their industry.

2.1

Not sure which industry to begin with? Look through this list and pick a few.

- Advertising/Media
- Aerospace/Defense
- Apparel
- Biotechnology
- Consumer Packaged Goods
- Distribution
- Financial Services
- Hospital & Healthcare
- Hospitality
- Manufacturing
- Professional Services
- Real Estate (Commercial/Residential)
- Retail
- Technology: Hardware, Software, Services
- Telecom
- Venture Capital/Private Equity

This is not meant to be an all-encompassing list. This is just something to get you started. Do a similar exercise that we talked about earlier. Pick a few industries, maybe five. Map out who you know in each industry. Through your networking, try to build an industry map of what that industry looks like. Think about the industry supply chain. Who are the suppliers, manufacturers, distributors, resellers/retailers, and service providers for that industry? Try to build a network around that supply chain.

You'll be amazed how similar you find the basic elements of each industry. Having a framework like this enables you to grasp the industry more clearly and better understand how each of the players fit.

Similar Business Models

Another way to look at building your network is to ask yourself the question: Who has a similar business model? If your supply chain looks like manufacturer to distributor to reseller/retailer to end user, you could be talking about the computer hardware industry or you could be talking about the food industry.

Automotive, computer hardware, and food industries share similar business models in that, until social media came about, the manufacturer rarely had much direct interaction with the users of its products.

Retailers and banks have similar business models in that they both typically have extensive brick-and-mortar locations. If you're running facilities management for a retailer, it would serve you to build some relationships with facilities managers for banks.

Your phone, internet, and television providers have extensive field service operations. Who else does? How about home healthcare? How about consumer appliances?

Having an overnight stay at a location that's not your own home? You could be in a hotel. You could be in a hospital. You could be at a university. You could be on a cruise ship. You could be in prison (let's hope you're not, though). What could people from each of these businesses learn from the other? Quite a bit, actually.

Here's an example of what you might do. Let's say you're in the banking industry and you'd like to connect with other people. You might target the following industries with similar business models, like those who also have brick-and-mortar locations where consumers are served. You might put together a target network like this:

2.1

Map out who you know. Fill in the gaps with who's missing.

1. Mark existing relationships with an X.
2. Mark desired relationships with an O.
3. Utilize those with an X, and others in your network, to get referred into those with an O.

Columns: Name, Company, Banking, Retail, Entertainment, Hospital, Restaurant.

Bernie Clark - Charles Schwab - Banking X
Ted Williams - Delaware North - Restaurant X
Tracy Tannenbaum - Banner Health - Hospital X
Tim Cook - Apple Computer - Retail X
Jamie Dimon - JPMorgan Chase - Banking O
Chris Costa - Goodwill Industries - Retail O
Jennifer Daniels - J Crew - Retail O
Adam Aron - AMC - Entertainment X

Business Model: Organizations with Brick & Mortar Locations

Name	Company	Banking	Retail	Entertainment	Hospital	Restaurant
Bernie Clark	Charles Schwab	X				
Ted Williams	Delaware North					X
Tracy Tannenbaum	Banner Health				X	
Tim Cook	Apple Computer		X			
Jamie Dimon	JPMorgan Chase	O				
Chris Costa	Goodwill Industries		O			
Jennifer Daniels	J Crew		O			
Adam Aron	AMC			X		

2.1

Maybe you decide after meeting with people in these areas you're more interested in those locations where people want to be served quickly. Therefore, maybe your restaurant category turns into fast food or quick service. Maybe your hospital category becomes more like outpatient surgicenters or dialysis locations. Maybe you take hotels off your target list. Your list can and should evolve along the way. Your list can and should evolve as you meet people and learn about what they're doing.

That's how you have to think about the value of your network. Think about what you could learn from others. Think about what you could share with others. You never really know until you start having conversations. The results are always enlightening.

These are only a few approaches: Competitive Forces, Functional Area, Industry, Business Model. You can build your network in whatever way you want. The key is to take action. *Do something!* Build it proactively versus reactively. Figure out who you want in your network and then go after them. Don't leave one of your most valuable assets up to chance.

Organizing your network

How do you keep your network organized? That's a great question. Your organization probably has a Customer Relationship Management (CRM) system for the sales team, but what about for everyone else? In a perfect world, the organization would extend that CRM system to everyone. In the less than perfect world we live in, you may want to use one of the many cloud-based online CRM systems, an Excel spreadsheet, or go old-school and use a piece of paper.

How do I find companies doing all of these things?

Let's say you've identified some functional areas, some industries, some companies, and some business models. Now what? It's time to find out about the things that exist under the radar. It's time to talk to people. But why would they talk to you, you ask? That's easy. Because you're going to ask. And you're going to ask in a way that will get you plenty of information.

Don't stop with the first person you meet. You don't have enough data to really know what's going on. You need to ask many people. Many, many people. I mean a lot of people! How many people? At least 25. Maybe 50. It might take 200. But you're going to get conversations with each and every one of them. You're going to learn what's going on. You're going to find out about the latest in a particular function; trends in an industry. You're going to get up to speed on the challenges the industry faces. You'll take a look at the players and find out who's doing what. You'll find out who are the suppliers, the buyers, the substitutes. You're going to figure out who's effective in which submarket and who's positioned for the coming years.

You're going to know a lot. Certainly a lot more than if you sat at your desk all day long. And with all of that information, you're going to be able to figure out how to make this information work…for others as well as yourself.

What if people want to know why you want to speak with them? Just tell them that you're looking to gain some insight on their industry/function/business model. You thought they'd be good people to speak with about that. Rarely do people think they have no insights to offer. For help on how to word these types of introductions, see Section 4.1 on Extending Networked Relationships and Getting a Meeting.

How long is this going to take? It could take months. It could take years. It could take a lifetime. It just depends on how much time you spend proactively doing the work. If you spend about two hours per month meeting with people, that's two to three people per month, and the potential foundation of 24 to 36 new relationships per year. As a general rule, a phone call might last 30 to 45 minutes. In person, 45 to 60 minutes. Meeting in person is almost always better and more memorable, but if your geographic location doesn't permit it, a phone call is an acceptable alternative. In case you're wondering, email and text are great for scheduling the logistics of the meeting (date, time, location), but not for the actual meeting. Never, ever let electronic communication take the place of a phone call or an in-person networking meeting.

Are you managing your relationships to produce the greatest returns?

Mike, a friend in New York, is a trader on the commodities exchange. He's been trading for more than 20 years, and success at trading comes naturally for him. Well, perhaps on the surface. It hasn't always been that way. When we get to talking about his early days as a trader, Mike recalls a time when he was pretty lousy at it, and came very close to quitting. Then one day, watching some senior traders, he started to see a pattern. They were heads down—managing each individual trade. Rarely did they come up for air to analyze their overall portfolio.

It was at that moment Mike had perfect clarity about what he was doing wrong and what he needed to do to be successful in the business. He'd been so caught up in analyzing his overall portfolio that he'd neglected the individual trades. He needed to quit worrying about the big picture and start drilling down on each individual trade. When he made each individual trade profitable, the entire portfolio would have a greater return on investment. Sounds pretty obvious in hindsight, right?

Mike's dilemma—and his solution—got me thinking about how most people proceed through life.

2.1

When you have a big project, they say to break it down. When you're learning to read and you have a three-syllable word in front of you, your teacher (or in my case, my sister Betsy) tells you to sound it out. This got me thinking about how people go after clients. We become so focused on the big picture—the monumental task of landing the perfect client—that we forget to drill down on the individual activities that will produce a greater return on investment—that is, new, incremental business.

If your organization is looking to expand its business, you might want to think about how you're approaching your prospecting. Are your teams so focused on landing a client that they're neglecting to manage the activities that will lead to that result? Does your process sound like this? *Let's see, I have to find some clients. Therefore, I have to meet as many people as possible. Therefore, I have to hand out as many business cards as I can. When someone asks me "How's business?" I will say "It could be better." With every conversation I will remind everyone that referrals are the greatest compliment.*

No, you don't! You don't have to do any of this, nor should you do any of this. If your organization is focused on conversations and activities like these, you're going to produce the worst returns ever recorded in history!

Start with the end in mind.

Why don't you start with the end in mind? How do you acquire a new client? No matter how much time your team spends at events, chances are good that without really meaningful interaction, new clients won't be lining up at the door anytime soon. At one point, your team will have to meet the right person at the right company and build the right relationship. How do you help them meet people, the right people? You think about where they spend their time. Where they network depends on what type of customer your organization wants.

Be interesting by being interested.

It's safe to say that if your team is meeting lots of people, building great relationships through smart questioning (remember Molly's Networking Rule #4: Be interesting by being interested), identifying needs/problems, and bringing insights to those organizations, its chances of being considered for opportunities should be great.

Your team needs to quit focusing on the activities that are inhibiting its ability to build relationships and start focusing on the ones that enable team members to build meaningful relationships. Manage these relationships carefully. Learn from each relationship and make improvements with the next one. Through this process, you'll be carrying on intelligent conversations about interesting problems that would be fascinating to solve. It won't take long before more clients start showing up. Once you've perfected this technique, the opportunities never stop. When you step back and take a look at the big picture, your overall portfolio of opportunities will show incredible returns. How's that for your very own bull market?

When I was looking to get into commercial real estate, I didn't know much about the industry. The bad news was that there was no book about it. The good news was that it seemed everyone I ran across knew someone in that very industry. I began scheduling meetings with anyone and everyone. I didn't care where they worked or what they did; if they were in the commercial real estate industry, I wanted to meet with them.

I asked the following questions, starting typically with the phrase:

2.1

Tell me a little bit about…

- *what you do.*
- *what types of people and companies you interact with.*
- *what types of firms are in this industry and what each one does.*
- *where your firm fits in the overall picture.*
- *who your biggest competitors are.*
- *your challenges.*

I'd also ask:

- *Who's doing interesting things?*
- *Who's expanding? Who's contracting? Why?*
- *Who are your largest customers?*
- *What about partnerships?*
- *Who are the people in the industry who are driving change? (Oh, do you know that person? Yes, I'd love to meet with them. Can you help me with that? Great!)*

- *Who are others I should meet with who will give me some great insight?*
- *What does it take to do your job effectively?*

Through this methodical line of questioning, I was able to map out the industry and identify the players with whom I wanted to develop a relationship. Throughout these conversations, I never forgot my Networking Rule #1: Networking is not about you. This helped me stay focused on bringing value to the people with whom I was meeting.

Is there such a thing as asking too many questions?

I suppose it's possible under the right conditions, but probably not. You certainly don't want to rattle off question after question without listening and taking each answer down the appropriate path. Be respectful of others' time and know when enough is enough. When my business partner Jay and I walked out of one of our first meetings together, he said, *Wow, you ask a lot of questions!*

I'm just trying to get them to talk, I told him. *The more they talk, the more we learn—and, honestly, the more they like us. The more they like us, the greater the possibility something will happen. If they don't like us, on the other hand, I can guarantee you nothing will happen.*

You never know to what level others will rise.

Back in 2002, I was invited to an event where Barbra Streisand was performing. My seat was in the nosebleeds, but I didn't really care. How often do you get to see Barbra Streisand perform for free? Prior to the performance, there was a social event where I happened to meet Adam, who had an extra ticket in the seventh row. Adam asked me if I wanted to join him. Of course I did! It was a great concert. David Foster was there (producer of the best holiday CD ever!) and Adam and I were introduced to a relatively unknown singer at the time named Michael Bublé. It was a great evening and I'd made a new friend. Well, two if you count Michael Bublé. At the time, Adam was the CEO of a group of resorts in Colorado. A few years later when I reached out to him, I found that he had left the resort company to start his own venture in the luxury travel business. Fast forward a few more years, and I was attempting to help someone get connected to Adam's prior resort firm in Colorado. I thought Adam would probably still know some people. I called the number I had for him, but it didn't work anymore, so I Googled him, only to find that he was no longer working on that travel venture. He was now part owner and CEO of a professional sports team. How exciting!

2.1

Now, some people would stop right there and say *This man is incredible. He's probably too busy to talk to me.* But how can you have a solid network if you don't focus on maintaining relationships? I decided to call the main line at a time when I thought there would be no gatekeeper. I pressed a bunch of buttons until I located the company directory. And on the second try, I reached Adam. And yes, he answered his phone himself.

Hi Adam, I said. *This is Molly Wendell.*

Before I had time to say, *Remember me?* Adam said, *Oh, hi Molly. I remember you.*

It had been a while since we'd last talked, but that doesn't mean anything. It's not as if his life was on hold waiting for my call. People have their own lives. People are living their lives. Reconnecting is generally a welcome interruption, as long as you're not reconnecting only when you need something.

When we met, did I think, *Oh, there's Adam, who will probably be an owner of a major sports team one day?* No, I thought, *This is an interesting person; we're having an interesting conversation. I'd like to stay in touch with this interesting person.* That's it.

How deep do you need to go?

It's one thing to know of or about someone, but an entirely different scenario to actually *know* someone. When you reach out, how quickly does the individual respond? How much do you know about this person's life other than her most recent position? How much time have you spent fostering the relationship at a time when you didn't need anything from him? How much time have you spent figuring out how to be of value to him? Without some level of ongoing communication, it's challenging to discern *how* to be of value.

Build the well before you need the water.

Let's return to Molly's Networking Rule #2 once again: Build the well before you need the water.

> I decide to reach out to a friend named Steve. Steve is impressive. I haven't spoken with him in a while and am curious about what he's been up to. Steve and I schedule a call to catch up. From that call, I learn that Steve is looking for some capital to back one of the companies he's interested in turning around. I have a few contacts in the world of capital and tell Steve I'll put him in touch with them. He is appreciative. I call one contact in particular, David, to let him know Steve will be in touch. It has been a few years since we've spoken. Turns

out David has just taken a new role at a fairly large company and he's looking to acquire some companies to expand their product line. After better understanding where they play, I come up with a few contacts for David. I can't guarantee these people will be able to help him. I know that if I don't connect them, we'll never know.

How many people can you help? How many people can you make connections for? Maybe, if you make an effort, you'll connect one person a week. One person a week, if you do it right, will likely turn into two or three more. Be thoughtful about who you connect with whom. People appreciate the value you place on their time; by not wasting it, they're more likely to appreciate you.

2.1

You might be thinking that you don't have time to do all the follow up. You don't have time to connect other people. You can't afford the time it takes to build a more solid network. Perhaps you can't afford *not* to.

What difference will all this connecting make in your life? A couple of things come to mind. First, being known as someone who knows people attracts more people to you. I've never heard anyone say, *Oh, yes, I definitely want to connect with Joe. I hear he knows absolutely no one.* Second, it's how you can get things done. Whether it's finding referrals for other people or finding referrals for your own business, being known in town helps your business in a positive way. Third, often times, the relationships you build transcend from business to personal and you find that people really care about your success. Who doesn't want that?

Remember, I'm not your customer, but I know your customer. And I know others who know your customer. Shouldn't you take the time to get to know me? Shouldn't you take the time to get to know them?

Building a network takes time. You might not know what the returns will be initially, but it's an investment in your future. If you make no investment, you can be sure your returns will reflect that.

2.1

The Networked Organization Action Plan

- Identify 20 people you'd like in your network: Company, Function, Industry, Business Model (five in each).

- Capture information in an online CRM tool, Excel spreadsheet, or on paper.

- Develop your questions to gain a better understanding of that functional area, industry, or business model.

- Make an effort to connect other people to each other.

2.1

Networking Through
Social Media
and "Corporate Social Branding"

Corporate Social Branding: CSB. Never heard of it before? That's because I made it up. It's a combination of Corporate Branding, Employer Branding, and Social Branding.

When you combine the marketing concept of Corporate Branding—promoting a brand name of a corporate entity, with the human resources concept of Employer Branding—the organization's efforts to communicate to its current and prospective employees that it is a desirable place to work, and Social Branding—using social technologies to communicate with social customers, their partners and constituents, or the general public—voilà, *Corporate Social Branding* is born.

How is your organization being viewed from an employee attractiveness standpoint? How is your organization being viewed from a potential customer attractiveness standpoint? How are you leveraging social media platforms like LinkedIn, Facebook, and

Twitter from a community standpoint? How do you take all three concepts and combine them into one consistent message across all audiences?

There's a great book called *The Discipline of Market Leaders* by Fred Wiersema and Michael Treacy that shows what it takes to not only become a leader in your market, but to stay there. It asks the question, *Which discipline are you: operational efficiency, customer service, or product excellence?* It talks about identifying what your organization does better than anyone else, and the unique value you provide. Market leaders major in one discipline and base all decisions on that discipline, while minoring in the other two. If Apple, a company known for its product excellence, for example, is making a decision to either invest in additional supply chain infrastructure and materials to meet 100% of the demand of a new product on launch day or put more money into the development of that product, the answer is simple: product development. It's not that Apple doesn't care about making sure the product will be available to everyone on day one, it's just that it cares more about creating a more innovative and leading edge product.

Take this concept and apply it to Corporate Social Branding. How are you aligning your market leadership discipline with your CSB?

Take a look at the chart on the following page. Think about your organization's market discipline. Think about the consistency of messaging in your Corporate Social Branding efforts. Create some tactics your team can implement that are in alignment with your CSB.

Market Leadership/Corporate Social Branding Alignment

Market Discipline	CSB Key Messages	Ideas/Examples that align with your CSB
Operational efficiency	The numbers; the results	Case studies with results
		Employee improvements
		Insight into efficiencies created for the customer benefit
Customer service	The human component/ solving the customer's problem	Customer testimonials on how the organization solved "my" problem; how to engage with the organization if you have that same problem
		Employee stories of how they solved problems for customers and why they love working for the organization
		Providing customers with a way to easily interact with you and your teams
Product excellence	Product innovation, the latest and greatest	Insight into R&D; what makes us tick
		Link to videos on how products are engineered/the design process
		Launch of new products, the problems they solve; why they're amazing

Leveraging social networking tools

Many organizations know that their online presence is made up of more than just their website; that it includes LinkedIn, Facebook, Twitter, and probably several other tools. Typical marketing efforts are focused on building consistent brands. The funny thing is that much of an organization's social presence is inconsistent. I looked at the LinkedIn and Facebook profiles of the 10 largest companies. Of the 10, only one had consistent messaging—and even on that one, you had to look really hard to find it. These are companies who likely have plenty of resources dedicated to ensuring their company is in the social media stratosphere. Yet their messages are all over the place. Maybe they have too many cooks in the kitchen?

2.2

Authentic social networking and branding

What does your organization's social branding look like? Does it enable your team to be more productive networkers?

What are you conveying to your stakeholders (current/prospective employees, current/prospective customers, suppliers, shareholders) in a consistent manner?

How are your messages consistent, whether in person, online, in media, or in writing?

Think about who you are, what you do, and for whom. Give an example and show that you've had results for your clients. Use the examples in the CSB grid as tactics you could employ in the social world to align your market discipline with your Corporate Social Branding efforts to attract and retain the right type of employees and customers.

Corporate social media communities started gaining traction soon after Facebook opened itself up to the rest of us and LinkedIn became popular. Many large organizations use social media for a variety of reasons. Deloitte uses Facebook heavily as a recruiting tool. IBM created not just an alumni community, but a full program devoted to the IBM network. It all started with a survey for IBM's ex-employees asking questions about their perceptions of IBM, and particularly how they felt about the company after being away from it. Flor Estevez, a person integral in the development of the program, and I spent some time discussing what IBM was trying to accomplish. It turns out that IBM was thinking about the value of those employees who'd left the company. While any company has its share of disgruntled employees, many people who left IBM still have very positive memories of their time there.

2.2

IBM realized that those people who left IBM with positive attitudes would make great ambassadors for its brand. These people were in IT decision making positions, had the influence of an IT decision maker, or, at a minimum, knew others who did. Imagine what could happen if you gathered the thousands upon thousands of previous employees and began a dialogue with them—in essence, creating an open line of communication. Letting them know what you're up to. Letting them interact with you. Letting them interact with each other. That's what the Greater IBM Connection is all about.

IBM was one of the first major companies to formally organize its ex-employees in such a way. Can you think of a better way to leverage people who aren't even on your payroll?

How are *you* engaging with your previous coworkers?

Better yet, how are you leveraging your own team?

The key is *consistency*. You want to be predictable so that what you say is what they expect. And, in turn, what they expect is what you deliver.

How your employees' social profiles affect your branding

How should an organization leverage its employees' social efforts… or should it? I'm not saying that managers should be trolling around their employees' LinkedIn, Twitter, and Facebook networks looking for business. I'm saying that if an employee is going to work for you, how do you want him or her to appear in the social media world?

2.2

What if organizations leveraged every employee's LinkedIn profile? Some managers worry when their employees spend too much time on their LinkedIn profiles. Smart companies, instead, are looking at the value of social tools and utilizing them in employee recruiting and lead generation efforts. Smart organizations want their employees to build valuable, authentic networks. Smart organizations guide employees on what kind of information they'd like to see on the employee profile, how they would like the organization viewed from a recruiting and lead generation standpoint. They spell out what a good customer looks like. As my good friend John Coyne always said, fill in the blanks: *We work with _____ who are struggling with _____.*

How about providing your **EMPLOYEES** training and guidelines that will make them appear more **PROFESSIONAL, RELEVANT, AND INTERESTING?**

How do you co-brand within the employee's profile?

What would you like your employees to include about the organization in their profiles? Although including good branding in an employee's profile should not be a big deal to any employee who's interested in staying, it can't be a mandate; it must be a suggestion. If you provide personal value in the form of training, your employees are much more likely to be receptive to the idea of including the organization's information in their profiles.

Provide them with a brief blurb about who they work for. Give them the opportunity to personalize it for themselves.

Maybe along the lines of, *What's great about working at* _____ *is*

_____ .

Give the rest of the world a little peek into your corporate culture. *Today, we're solving* _____ .

Maybe it's something like, *I'm currently/I just finished working on*

_____ .

How can you attract future employees and customers by giving them a glimpse of what you're doing today? Update it. Keep it fresh.

I can hear the complaints now. *You mean to tell me that my company has the right to put information in my LinkedIn Profile?* No, they don't, and that's not what I'm saying. But if you're proud to work there, wouldn't you want you and your company to be positioned in the best way possible? If you're not proud to work there, maybe it's time to move on.

If you have an exciting success, why not have all the employees share the news with their networks in the form of a status update? This can't be like Throwback Thursday and managed on a schedule.

It should happen when it happens, but it must be well thought out, short, and sweet. Maybe include a picture or video or one line with a logo. Maybe talk about some kind of impressive result: where the client was able to get to market faster or reduce costs by X percent. If you can't name the client due to confidentiality issues, name the industry and size of the organization (e.g., a large insurance firm, a regional hospital, a bank). When you do this, be sure to give your employees more information and a follow-up process in case someone in their network wants to learn more.

LinkedIn could be one of the biggest branding opportunities, but most organizations are missing out. How about providing your employees training and guidelines that will make them appear more professional, relevant, and interesting? Some companies might be afraid to teach LinkedIn for fear that its employees will jump ship. If employees are interested in looking elsewhere, they will, but one foot out the door is still one foot in the door. Treat your employees right. Don't give them a reason to look elsewhere. If teaching them how to use and leverage LinkedIn causes them to leave, perhaps the organization has more systemic issues that ought to be addressed.

I'm on LinkedIn. Now what do I do?

Let's say you've embraced the idea of getting everyone on the same page when it comes to LinkedIn. You've had your employees set up a profile. They have some references. They've uploaded a bunch of contacts. They're ready to go.

Not so fast.

Set up a professional photographer for the day to photograph your employees. Make it fun. Make it interesting. Please don't make it look like a selfie in a poorly lit room against a yellow wall. Have a computer available on the spot where the employees can upload the picture to their profile right away or, better yet, have someone there to do it for them. When it comes to figuring out a feature on LinkedIn, it's a lot faster for one person to do something a thousand times than for a thousand people to do it one time.

As for the actual wording, many books and websites exist to help you with your profile. The main idea here is that you want to ensure it's not boring. Don't simply copy and paste bios. Don't load resumes. Never write in the formal third person. *Mr. Smith worked in the technology industry…*blah blah blah. Be real. Be interesting. Be authentic. What kind of impression do you want to make? Which accomplishments do you want people to remember about you? How do you want to position yourself for the past, present, and future?

Once you have your profile up and some connections, it will snowball. After six months, you could probably double the size of your network without proactively requesting one single connection. But again, think about who you want in your network. Just because someone requests to connect with you doesn't mean you should agree to connect with them. Think about how authentic you want your network to be.

One thing you ought to do on a regular basis is go through your connections—on LinkedIn or otherwise—and reach out to a few people. I don't mean by emailing them with something like *I'm checking in*, but by actually placing a phone call. See what they're up to. See if there's any way you can help them. Maybe provide a contact or two. While the contact may seem random to the receiver, it doesn't have to be random to you. Have a plan. Make a plan. Get proactive about your relationships. Get proactive about cultivating those relationships to get deeper.

Remember the story of Tom, who only reached out to Wally when he needed help? Are you that person—only reaching out through social media when you need something? Stop being that person right now.

Another thing to do is regularly mine your LinkedIn connections. Take a look and see who's connected with whom. Of your friend's connections, with whom would you like to form a relationship? Again, don't email them. Pick up the phone. Catch up. Figure out how you can provide value to that person. Then, ask about the connection. Don't be discouraged if people don't actually know all of their connections. Sometimes people connect online with those they don't know. Shocking, I know. That's their choice. Maybe while you have them on the phone, you can ask about someone else in their network.

Employees and companies have an incredible opportunity to embrace and leverage Corporate Social Branding. Don't just throw something up and see if it sticks. Do it strategically. Do it proactively. Do it thoughtfully. Do it consistently.

The Networked Organization Action Plan

- Create/Modify LinkedIn profile.
- Create your own authentic social network by inviting a couple of new connections per week.
- Contact at least one person per week to say hello, see what they're up to, and figure out how you can help them.
- Before connecting with someone, ask yourself the following questions:
  - *Who is this person?*
  - *Have I ever met him/her in person before?*
  - *How do I know him/her?*
  - *Am I confident that having this person in my network will be a positive reflection of me?*
- Develop a co-branding strategy with your employees.

2.2

111

REAL WORLD NETWORKING

3.1

Networking:
That First Impression

| Realizing Molly's Networking Rule #1

Networking is not about you.

We've talked a lot about why building relationships is important and how to build your network. We've also discussed the difference between efficient and effective results. Now we're going to delve into specific ways to ensure your networking efforts are the most effective possible.

But first, let's remember Molly's Golden Rule of Networking: *It's not about you.* It's about everyone else but you. That's why we're going to spend a lot of time on how to make the interaction more comfortable for the *other* person. Over time, you'll start to see how the more you make it comfortable for others, the more comfortable and enjoyable the experience will be for you.

You never get a second chance to make a first impression.

I've met very few people who admit to actually enjoying the traditional experience of networking. I've met just as few who think they're pretty good at it. Either way, my experience is that most people could use some help not only in fine-tuning, but also in the basics. Because when you're out there, the first thing you do is create an impression. It's not one thing that makes up that first impression, it's all the little things. The goal is to do all the little things right to make that first impression a good one. Take Shelby.

Shelby is easy for me to remember because he is probably the most offensive person I've ever met. I am at an event catching up with a friend named Joe. Normally, I try not to spend too much time with people I already know, but I haven't seen Joe in a while and it's nice to reconnect. Shelby walks up, interrupts our conversation, introduces himself, shoves his business card in my face, and tells me he wants to get together for lunch. What's wrong with this picture? Pretty much everything!

First of all, Joe is in the middle of a story when Shelby interrupts. Then, Shelby gives me a lousy handshake. Completely oblivious to the fact that Joe and I had been deep in conversation, Shelby hijacks it with no sense of personal or professional etiquette. He assumes I actually want his business card before I even have the chance to figure it out for myself. And, finally, an invitation to lunch with someone who leaves me with a bad first impression is not the least bit appealing.

What do I do? I'll tell you what I don't do. I don't give him my card, nor give him any way to get in touch with me. I simply smile politely and wait for him to move on to the next group.

It's sad, really, because Shelby might be great. Shelby might be someone I ought to know. But I'll never find out, because I can't get beyond that overwhelmingly poor first impression.

What can you do to make your first impression the best it can possibly be? So much. Start with the basics—the little things that, all combined, make up that first great, lasting impression. And be sure to take into account the factors that detract from that first great, lasting impression.

Here are a few of the little things in networking that affect the first impression. We'll look at each one separately:

- nametags
- great handshakes
- business cards
- your introduction
- notecards

Nametags

You might be wondering why nametags warrant entire paragraphs of discussion. You might be wondering why they could possibly be so important. Here's why.

When you put on a nametag at an event, the whole point is to make it easier for others to remember your name. Very few people are great at remembering names. So, don't feel bad if someone doesn't remember yours. We're fortunate that most meeting planners provide nametags for that very reason.

When filling out your nametag, be sure to put your first and last name. How many times have you been to an event to see Bob on a nametag…and that's it? Who does he think he is? Cher? Madonna? Usher? How many Bobs will there be at any given event? Plenty.

Wear your nametag on the right side of your chest—opposite your heart. Why do you do this? When shaking hands, it provides a line of sight to your name, and when people see your name and hear your name, they're more likely to remember your name. Remember, networking is about everyone but you, so whatever you can do to make life easier for the other person, that's what you should do.

Sometimes people try to be unique and wear their nametag on their waist or in the middle of their shirt. I guess they want to be known for being different. Be known for being professional, not the weirdo who wore his nametag on his forehead.

Be sure to use a Sharpie® marker to write your name. Not only do people have bad memories, but they generally have pretty bad eyesight. Writing your name in light pen, or worse, pencil, ensures you're not doing anything to make it easier for others. Clear writing allows people, from a distance, to see your name. If they can't read the name on your nametag, you're less likely to be remembered—other than being remembered as the guy whose name they couldn't remember.

What do you do if there is no Sharpie? Good networkers are prepared. They bring their own. Always. You never know when the event planners might forget to bring a supply. Plus, you never know when you'll meet someone famous and want to get his autograph.

I'm on an airplane traveling from Los Angeles to Phoenix. I sit down in first class and glance at my seat-mate. Hmm, I think I know him from somewhere. I think he might be famous. I start the conversation the same way I begin every airplane conversation. Are you coming or going? Are you going home or going away? He tells me he is headed to Phoenix on business. I ask what kind of business and he says the movies.

Okay, now I really think he might be famous. I ask how long he's been in the movies. *About 50* years, he says. Okay, I'm an idiot. He is absolutely famous. So, I say what I say when I don't know what to say. *Do you love it?* Yes, he does. I proceed to ask him how he got started and he tells me he went to Michigan State University to play football. As he puts it, they sent him home his freshman year in a body bag. He decided against another year of being a tackling dummy and started taking acting classes at a university in New York. The rest was history. About 20 minutes into the flight, I realize I'm sitting next to the actor James Caan.

Oh, my gosh! James Caan on my right. Sharpie in my purse. How do I get the two of them to meet? It takes some quick thinking and lots of questions, but I finally figure out a reason for him to give me his contact information. My friend, Stephanie, is trying to get her first film produced. She isn't from Hollywood. I ask Jimmy if he might know someone who can help her. Of course he does, and of course he'd be glad to help her. When it comes time to write down his contact information, I have him do it. James Caan, say hello to my little friend the Sharpie. Voilà! Autograph and phone number all in one. Genius!

The handshake

What does your handshake say about you? I've had people get mad at me for advising them about how to correctly shake a hand. What makes me an expert? I've been on the receiving end of thousands upon thousands of handshakes and the majority of them have been less than impressive. I've analyzed in great detail what works and what doesn't. So, take my advice and let me give you some guidance as to what makes up a professional, quality handshake.

> At a networking training class for executives, one of the attendees from Google shakes my hand. I tell him, *Jim, you shake hands like you're about to attack me. Your arm swoops in at full-speed. It's a little intimidating. Is that your intention? No,* says Jim, *not at all! But it's funny you say that because I've been told I can appear intimidating and I've never been sure why people thought that.*
>
> Well, now we know.

When I'm speaking to groups, I often test handshakes looking for ones that are good. In a room of 100 people, I'm lucky if I find five people who have a professional, quality handshake. I usually find at least one person who is so mad at me for criticizing his handshake that he complains to the organizer. I'm just trying to help. I'm just trying to ensure that he won't be the person who's spoken about in the women's restroom. Did you shake that guy's hand? Talk about creepy with a capital C!

That conversation is happening more than you know.

Do you really want to be that guy?

Maybe you have sweaty palms. Do you have any idea what it's like to be on the receiving end of a sweaty-palm handshake? The bigger issue here is that no one knows if it's simply a case of sweaty palms. For all we know, you just came from the restroom. I don't even want to think about that!

Oh, and this really should go without saying: when you walk into an event, use your left hand to carry anything you bring with you and have the right one handshake-ready. Nothing is more awkward

3.1

than shaking someone's left hand. Okay, some things are more awkward, but the left-handed shake is pretty high up there on the awkward scale.

For every one person who doesn't appreciate my criticism of his or her handshake, at least 99 appreciate the fact that I teach them a handshake that is considered universally accepted. This is just about the time that some "culturally enriched" person will tell me that in some countries it's considered rude to shake hands. Thanks for the lesson in global culture. I've traveled to more than 50 countries and found very few people worldwide who did not welcome me with an overly enthusiastic handshake. I'm not saying I'm right. I'm just saying that handshakes are more common than people realize. And yes, I know, it's practically sacrilegious to touch someone's hand in some countries. Let's just agree for the purposes of this handshake discussion that I'm not referring to those countries.

There's a time and place to be memorable. The handshake is not one of them. Don't be known for a different handshake. Nobody appreciates it when you turn their wrist to put your hand on top. Nobody wants you to crunch their knuckles and remind them of the pain their older brother George caused them all those years. Nobody likes the grandma handshake…not even your grandma!

Use the same handshake for everyone you meet. That way, you'll either offend everyone or no one. Hopefully no one. Here are the steps of a universally (or at least domestically) accepted handshake:

1. *Extend arm.*
2. *Use a firm, but not too tight, grip.*
3. *Make eye contact.*
4. *Smile (if you can without looking creepy).*
5. *Double-pump your arm.*
6. *Let go. Please, please, please know when to let go.*

You're probably thinking this is ridiculously simple. Bingo. A good handshake is ridiculously simple, but when you become aware of the handshake you'll start to recognize all those little things that don't work in a handshake. Sometimes people don't extend their arm enough, or they wiggle their elbow like they're doing the chicken dance at a wedding. You think that looks professional? Sometimes people who are seated try to shake a person's hand who is standing. If the other person is standing, you need to stand up as well before you begin the handshake.

Most people either grip too loosely or too tightly. A woman I know has the firmest grip of any handshake I've ever experienced. You know what she's saying. *I'm tough and I could kill you.* At least that's what I read into it. Do you think I want to be her friend? Not a chance. She could kill me.

3.1

One of my biggest pet peeves is when people shake my hand without making eye contact. It feels so insincere. This happens weekly at church. While I don't correct people at church, I think we'd be a better, more engaged congregation if the few times we interacted with each other during the service we actually made eye contact with the person with whom we were engaging.

Most people either single-pump or triple-pump. Some people who have moved to the U.S. from another country sometime after 18 years of age tend to keep pumping until your arm gushes oil. Sometimes people stop pumping, but still hold onto your hand as if you're dating or something. Nothing's worse than wearing out your welcome in the handshake. If you think you've held on too long, the answer is yes, you have.

You might think that something so seemingly simple as a handshake is not a big deal, but it is. If it's uncomfortable, if it's awkward, you can be sure it does nothing to add to a positive first impression. And though it's not impossible, it's definitely very difficult to recover from a negative first impression.

The business card

Here's my big advice on the business card. Carry them in a nice case…and never hand them out. This seems counterintuitive, but it is actually very strategic. Here's the reality. He who holds the card holds control of the conversation. If you give people your card and you don't get theirs, they are in complete control of the conversation—what, where, when—or if it's even happening at all.

Get their card. Maintain control.

> He who holds the card holds
> # CONTROL
> of the
> ## CONVERSATION.

Have you ever received a card from someone that looks like it's the last one of its kind? Bent corners covered in purse or pocket lint surrounded by coffee stains, with the bearer saying *This is my last card.* Let's hope so. Let's hope you don't have more like this! Honestly, if this is what your last card looks like then you don't have a card. You're completely out. Because, again, this goes back to the impression. Hand me a filthy card and I think you're not as professional as someone who hands me a clean card. One time, I was going through the cards on my desk when I found one that was really small—about 1" x 2". It was obvious that it had been cut to this size from the normal business card. Then I remembered that I'd met this man on a plane. He'd been all out of cards and ended up giving me the card he'd cut and inserted into his luggage tag. Now that's some seriously dedicated networking!

I could have easily just given him my card and had him follow up with me, but then I would have handed over control of the conversation.

Here are a couple things to keep in mind about your cards:

- Keep them stored in a good card case to ensure they stay free from lint and stains.

- Have them handy when you go to a networking event. It's not a good use of time watching you dig through your purse for 10 minutes searching for your ever elusive card case among all of the items that will win you money on *Let's Make a Deal:* "Fifty dollars right now for someone who has a jumbo paper clip and a car wash receipt in her purse."

3.1

- Never hand out a card unless someone specifically asks for it. I've been to many an event where everyone at my table passes around business cards, usually followed by someone saying to no one in particular, *Oh, are we doing this? Okay, let me send my cards around.* Tell me why it's so important that the person you sat across the table from—the same person with whom you had zero conversation whatsoever—would need your card? Why would that person want your card? Maybe they want to put you on their weekly email newsletter list. Is that what you want? Did you make such a great impression talking to other people that they actually want to get to know you? Or are they just too polite to not take your card? Either go up afterward and introduce yourself, build a relationship, and possibly exchange cards, or take a pass. Don't ever send cards around the table without knowing exactly who will be receiving one.

Cards used to be expensive. Not so much anymore. Perhaps you should act as if they're very expensive because there is a cost to your time and your time is valuable. You don't get points for handing out the most cards. Putting your contact information in the wrong hands could cost you a lot of time. It's hard enough keeping track of the cards you do ask for. Why would you want to keep track of the cards you don't ask for?

The Networked Intro: One on one

Another thing that can take your first impression down a notch or two is how you introduce yourself. Unfortunately, networking events are typically where you find people who show up and throw up. It's not pretty. Take Bill, for example.

I met Bill at an event. Bill runs some kind of financial services company. Bill went on and on about his firm. I'd tell you all about it but I was so bored in the first 15 seconds that I quit listening. Bill kept on going for about another 15 minutes.

It reminds me what my friend Dean Del Sesto always says, *Enough about me. Let's talk about you. What do you think about me?*

Some call it a 30-second elevator pitch. I call it a two-second intro and most people are pretty challenged when it comes to creating it, let alone delivering it. Everyone wants to get a pitch in, but the problem is that most people don't know how to position their pitch in a way that makes them memorable.

There's a great story in the book *Made to Stick* about a journalism class Nora Ephron, famed screenwriter, attended.

Ephron started her career as a journalist and still remembers the first day of her journalism class. Although the students had no journalism experience, they walked into their first class with a sense of what a journalist does: A journalist gets the facts and reports them. To get the facts, you track down the five W's—who, what, where, when, and why.

As students sat in front of their manual typewriters, Ephron's teacher announced the first assignment. They would write the lead to a newspaper story. The teacher reeled off the facts. "Kenneth L. Peters, the principal of Beverly Hills High School, announced today that the entire high school faculty will travel to Sacramento next Thursday for a colloquium in new teaching methods. Among the speakers will be anthropologist Margaret Mead, college president Dr. Robert Maynard Hutchins, and California governor Edmund 'Pat' Brown." The budding journalists sat at their typewriters and pecked away at the first lead of their careers. Ephron and most of the other students produced leads that reordered the facts and condensed them into a single sentence: "Governor Pat Brown, Margaret Mead, and Robert Maynard Hutchins will address the Beverly Hills faculty Thursday in Sacramento…blah, blah, blah."

3.1

The teacher collected the leads and scanned them rapidly. Then he laid them aside and paused for a moment.

Finally, he said, "The lead to this story is 'There will be no school next Thursday.'"

"It was a breathtaking moment," Ephron recalls. "In that instant I realized that journalism was not just about regurgitating the facts, but about figuring out the point. It wasn't enough to know the who, what, when, and where; you had to understand what it meant. And why it mattered."

This begs the question, why do *you* matter? What do you mean when you tell me what you do, and what does it matter, and to whom? Give us the lead story.

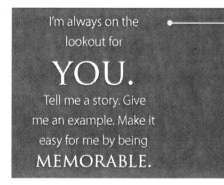

I'm always on the lookout for

YOU.

Tell me a story. Give me an example. Make it easy for me by being MEMORABLE.

Your two-second commercial should paint a picture in someone's mind of what you do and for whom. Even if what you do is easily understood, giving an example helps us remember it more because we can visualize the idea in our head. People remember the stories. People remember the pictures.

Here's an example of what usually happens:

Molly: *Hi John, what do you do?*

John: *I work for Data Synthesis.*

Molly: *Oh, what does Data Synthesis do?*

John: *We filter data through a series of formulas and equations to determine the best possible alternatives and then make recommendations.*

Molly: *Sounds impressive, but I'm not sure I really understand exactly what you do.*

Or, it could go something like this:

Molly: *Hi John, what do you do?*

John: *I work for Data Synthesis.*

Molly: *Oh, what does Data Synthesis do?*

John: *We work with marketing departments helping them analyze all of their data. When Coca-Cola is trying to figure out how to utilize all of the data they've collected in their Under-the-Cap game, we take that data and figure out the people who are most likely to buy Coke only when it's on sale. We email them different coupon amounts and measure which ones they redeem. How about you, Molly? What do you do?*

Get the picture?

Maybe that's not all you do, but given that it's the first time we've met, do I really need to know everything that you do as a person and organization? Give me one story the first time I meet you. Then, the next time I see you, give me another one. When we meet other people, I'll likely use one of those stories as a way to introduce you.

People always have a story bottled up, but they usually don't even think to use it. What two or three stories could you use to summarize what you do and the firm you work for? When you're a smaller company it's probably best to drop a big company name as a customer. I have a friend whose company does business with Facebook. Of all the companies it does business with, Facebook is probably the smallest customer in terms of revenue, but certainly the largest in terms of recognition. It's an easy one to rattle off because people can relate to it. And when they can relate, it's easier for them to remember.

Once you've finished your quick intro, you should immediately jump to a question that gets the other person talking, something like *And how about yourself?* Actually, I'd prefer if you did this before telling your story. Too many people go to networking events assuming everyone is there to listen to them. Don't assume everyone, or even anyone, is there to listen to you. Do assume you are there to listen to everyone else. The one person you know the most about is you. How much more information do you need to know about you? Probably not a lot. How much talking about you do you need to do at your next event? Probably not much.

What if you did something crazy...like not tell them about your business, and instead focus completely on them and their business?

What if you just deflected the *What do you do?* question like this? *I'm in finance. How about yourself, Mike?*

Try turning the conversation back to focusing on them as quickly as possible. And then ask more questions to get them talking.

Why is it important to ask all of the questions? You know the answer. The more people talk about themselves, the more they like you. The more they like you, the more they open up their network to you. Again, this is not new news. This is age-old advice from Dale Carnegie in *How to Win Friends and Influence People*. Even though Dale's been talking about this since the 1930s, it's not outdated. It still works! Many people don't practice this concept. Many people show up and throw up. And these are usually the same people who think they've had great success at a networking event because they passed out 30 cards and told just as many people all about themselves. That approach just doesn't work.

How do you tell if your approach is working? People will help you when you need it. People are there for you when you have the occasional request. People begin referring you to others without being prompted.

The Networked Intro: One on many

When you have the opportunity to introduce yourself to the entire room, are you seizing the moment? I was working with a financial services firm who sponsored many events. Not once did they prepare their local people for any time at the microphone. These people were left on their own to come up with something to say. It's not that they weren't capable, it's just that most people don't plan ahead, and what could be a clear, concise, consistent, and memorable message turns into a stumbling, drawn-out series of words that makes little sense to anyone. When we hand over the microphone, it's obvious who has prepared and who hasn't. We don't want to see another 10-minute presentation. We want to hear about you and remember you.

When you're at an association event, attending a functional event, or sponsoring an event, always be prepared to take advantage of the fact that at one point everyone's attention may just be focused on you. Will your time be worthwhile or wasted?

I liken this to delivering a speech at the Oscars. When someone is nominated for Best Actor, he'd better have some words prepared. With the chances being about one in five, it's pretty good odds that he might win. Yet, how many times have you watched an awards show where it's obvious the winner didn't prepare? This is rarely true of the Best Writer. They know how to write, whether it's a screenplay or a speech. They plan ahead, and it shows. Take your cue from the Best Writer. Plan ahead.

The chance to own the floor, if only for a minute, during someone else's meeting is quite powerful. Too many people squander their opportunity to make a better impression, attract a new customer, or even find a friend. Not only

> When introducing yourself to a group
> # BE BRIEF.
> # BE BOLD.
> # BE GONE.

3.1

should you be focused on who else is in the room, you should also be focused on what you should be saying. And name, rank, and serial number just won't cut it.

What should you think about when faced with this great opportunity? Think about the key messages you want to articulate. Think about where you need help. If a potential customer were in the room, what would you say; how would you say it; how could you say it in a way that makes them want to learn more? Most of all, think about how you can get as many people as possible to want to meet you afterward—to proactively seek you out. The closer you can get to a conversation instead of a presentation, the better.

Feedback, in the form of results, is fairly immediate. By the end of the evening, if no one comes up to you, you must've said the wrong thing to the wrong people at the wrong time. Essentially, a marketing failure. If one or two people come up to you afterward, you know you're headed in the right direction. If it's more than that, you should be thrilled. If the people coming up to you are actually people you want to get to know as well, then your little spiel worked like a charm.

I am in a meeting full of very impressive businesswomen. At one point during the meeting, every woman stands up and takes the time to introduce herself. In this case, out of the 50 other people in the room, I know only two—which means 48 chances to make a good first impression. I have to figure out what information I want to get across. First and foremost, I want to let all the executives in the room know that I speak at corporate conferences on the topic of building relationships. And when I'm not at a speaking engagement, I do executive search, helping companies fill the gaps in their executive teams. And, oh, I work with global executives on teambuilding and coaching. Sounds like a mouthful. But I've figured out a way to present the information in a clear, concise and entertaining way.

At the end of the meeting, I have more than 10 business cards from people who want to meet with me. Out of those, four are people whose names, based on their intros, are ones I've written down that I want to meet.

Are all of these people potential customers? Maybe not. But do they all have the ability to refer me? Maybe.

3.1

131

Have you ever gotten caught off guard in a situation like this? Sometimes, most times, you'll just have a minute or two to create some customization around your message. A canned intro or memorized elevator speech isn't going to get you the same results. It makes you sound stiff and rehearsed. Words that are authentic, targeted, with elements inspired in the moment are the ones that achieve the results you want. So, remember: Be brief. Be bold. Be gone.

Some elements you might use in your intro:

- a hook; points 1 and 2; close
- a story (people are more likely to remember it)
- enthusiasm (a smile)
- a reason for people to seek you out
  - a problem you're trying to solve
  - some insight/help you'd love to gain

3.1

Be prepared.
Always be ready to take notes.

I am constantly amazed at the number of people who show up at a networking event completely unprepared.

I am having a conversation with Joe. An interesting person, Joe works for a semiconductor company in its automotive division. His company is currently figuring out how automotive manufacturers can incorporate its technology into music systems, sound decks, and all things entertainment. I guess focusing on driving just isn't enough anymore. Specifically, Joe is looking to acquire companies with innovative technology.

A couple of months ago, I'd happened to meet someone who was working on some innovative technology in that same area. Perhaps it would benefit them to know each other? I tell Joe about this company and the person I met, and that they ought to connect. Joe tells me he'll follow up with me. I ask Joe if he wants to write the person's name down, and perhaps write mine down as well. Joe doesn't have a pen or a piece of paper. Really Joe, no pen or paper? Did you just come to this event for the food? Instead, he says, *That's okay, I'll remember it.* No offense, Joe, but I have a strong feeling that after you polish down that second drink, meet seven other people, and catch up with some friends, you're not going to remember much. I'll do you a favor and write it down for you. I pull out my stash of NetNotes™ (Networking Note Cards), write down the details, and hand it back to Joe. Now, he can choose to follow up…or not. His call.

3.1

Some of you may be wondering why Joe didn't just ask for my card. Sometimes I don't carry cards. Maybe secretly I'm testing everyone to see if they're prepared with pen and paper. I'm more interested in determining if I want your card than giving you mine. Or are you one of the people saying, *That would never happen to me, I have a great memory.* So do I, but why chance it? If you write it down, you can free up your mind to remember something else, like the name of the person you just met.

The next time you go to a networking event—and by the way, every day in life is a networking event—even those times that don't appear at first glance to be networking events like grocery shopping, having a pedicure/haircut, sitting on an airplane, standing in line…any line—make sure you're prepared. Always have pen and paper with you. Never be left without the ability to write!

You can download your very own NetNotes at mollywendell.com.

Remember, it's the little things.

Yes, it's all the little things that make up that one first, lasting impression. It's not that you can't make a great impression without taking any of what I'm saying into consideration; it's just that you can make a better impression when you do. Your nametag, handshake, business card, introduction, and preparedness all say you're ready for anything.

Hopefully, by practicing these basic ideas, you'll never need a second chance. Why? Because you made a great, lasting impression the first time.

3.1

The Networked Organization Action Plan

- Get business cards instead of giving business cards.

- Master the handshake.

- Develop your basic intro; think of stories/examples.

- Download NetNotes from mollywendell.com.

3.1

3.2

Networking
Events

| Realizing Molly's Networking Rule #3

Be there and aware.

I had just gotten back from a really great Executives Network Happy Hour in San Francisco. What made it so great was the interesting conversation. Conversation that only benefited those in the room. That got me thinking. How many conversations are we missing because we're not in the room?

How many **CONVERSATIONS** are you **MISSING** because you're **NOT IN THE ROOM?**

Getting out there forces you to bring your "A" game, to step up your professionalism. If you're sitting at home, hanging out online—sending emails and *networking* electronically—it's really easy to get lazy. After all, the dog doesn't care if you ever change out of your pajamas. But stepping out into the world, and I mean physically, gives you the opportunity to have the kind of personal interaction that humans so desperately need. If there's one thing our society is losing, it's the personal, face-to-face, one-on-one interaction. The kind where you can practice your conversational skills, hone your ability to listen, read non-verbal cues, take conversations to new directions, and see how interested and interesting you and your peers really are.

But be forewarned. If you're going to actually attend an event, you need to make a commitment to be there. And I mean *really* be there. How many conversations are you missing because you show up physically, but not mentally?

In this section, we'll talk about how to make the most of traditional networking events.

Go early. Stay late.

3.2

Once you've made the decision to attend an event, you might as well take full advantage of it. Maximize your opportunity to meet as many people as you can and have as many interesting conversations as possible. If you're only there for an hour, you might have three 20-minute conversations. But what if you stayed an extra hour? Maybe you could meet twice as many people and have twice as many interesting conversations.

Don't forget about the impression you're making.

If you're wearing your Bluetooth headset, take it off prior to walking in. It's really distracting because we're not sure if you're talking to us or someone else.

If you're negative, you're not interesting. Be happy, be positive. Be excited about the possibility that you might meet someone new, learn something fascinating about him or her, have something in common. Jobs come and go. Friendships can last forever.

If you're always talking about work or the fact that you're out of work, the truth is you're really kind of boring. I used to be in an industry where everyone talked about the same thing at every event. The industry. Their first question was always the same: *How's business?* One of two answers work for that question. Good or bad. Once you get that out of the way, there isn't much left to talk about. The people were nice. The conversation was painful.

Focus on getting to know someone personally: where they're from, what they like to do, things they're involved in. Start building a relationship and see where it goes. You might find you have much in common and end up making a new friend!

Get out there. Step it up. Engage in interesting, meaningful conversation. Ask smart questions. Make new friends. And stop letting the conversations go on without you!

Let's go meet some people.

One of the easiest ways to build your network and maximize your opportunities is to attend networking events. How many? It depends. How serious are you about building your network?

How do you find the events? On any given day, all you have to do is look online, open the newspaper, or ask around to find out what's happening. You can bet there will be a breakfast, lunch and/or dinner/happy hour event virtually every day of the week.

With so many out there, which ones should you attend? Go back to your target list—the one you put together when we talked about Building Your Relationship Portfolio. Look at where you have gaps and use events as a way to fill in those gaps.

You'll want to have a good balance of all types of events. Of course you'll go to events in your own industry, but also venture out to see what's going on in other industries. You'll be surprised how much there is to learn from other industry perspectives.

Go to events in your functional area as well as others. Think about building a more diverse network, not sticking only to those that focus on the same thing you do. Go to other business events in your community that attract people from all industries and functional areas.

Test out a few events to see if you're meeting the types of people you'd like. Typically, you don't have to be a member of the organizations to attend their events. And don't forget charity events. They tend to attract a diverse crowd.

Morning or evening events

Depending on whether you're a morning person or a night person, you'll probably gravitate toward certain types of events. Typically, morning events are breakfast meetings and often have a speaker. You'll have a brief amount of time to network before and after breakfast. These events are great if you're uncomfortable working a room. The key here is to utilize the time before and after to meet people. Arrive early, and don't rush off right after the breakfast. Some of the best connections can be made lingering after the meeting.

Evening events tend to be more of a social setting, and because of that, typically you'll have the opportunity to meet more people. Morning events are not better than evening ones. Evening events are not better than morning ones. Morning people like morning events. Night people like night events. Regardless of which type of person you are, be sure to attend a combination of both types. Morning people need to get to some evening events. Night people need to get to some morning events. That way, you meet people you wouldn't normally meet if you only attend the events at the time of day toward which you naturally gravitate.

Whether you go to a morning, lunchtime, or evening event, remember this: It all happens in the last 15 minutes. Whatever "it" is, that's when it happens. Don't be so eager to rush off that you miss "it."

How much of the conversation are you missing because you're doing all of the talking?

3.2

My dad is having chest pains, so my mom calls 911. When the paramedics arrive, they start to ask Dad some questions. But Dad has other ideas. *Hey,* he says. *Do you know Willie?* Willie is the fire chief. Turns out the paramedics work for him. *What about Mark?* Mark is their immediate boss. It's amazing. In the midst of crisis, Dad is making conversation, finding common bonds. *Networking.* I think this earns Dad a little extra attention.

Fast forward to the hospital. We're in with my dad, waiting to hear from the doctor. As a general rule, Dad never seems to know what's wrong with him or what they're going to do. And now I know why. Just as the doctor is about to share some

> very important information, Dad interrupts with his own very important questions. *Did you get a chance to see the Auburn game last night? Are you a golfer? Darly sure is a great nurse, isn't she? Do you know Jim—yeah, over in Telemetry? He's really something!* And that's when it occurs to me. How much is Dad missing because he is too busy talking and not busy enough listening?

This gets me thinking about people who are networking. You might be having a conversation with somebody, and just when they're about to share some really important information, you interrupt with something you're dying to say. By saying it, you take the conversation in another direction, and now you'll never know what it was this person was going to tell you. It could have been a possible connection. It could have been a lead. It could have resulted in some real revenue. But instead, you felt compelled to talk.

Sometimes it's that anxious start/stop feeling where you're waiting for an opening so you can interject. Actually, it's kind of like jumping rope. You keep waiting your turn, and if the timing isn't perfect, you end up getting tangled in the rope. The anticipation of getting your timing just right forces you to think more about you and what you need to say, rather than listening to them and finding out what you need to hear. Next time you're about to get tangled in the rope, jot down a reminder and then continue listening.

Don't confuse a networking event with a personal monologue: act accordingly.

People do this all the time. They talk and talk and then talk some more. But to be a good conversationalist, and therefore good at building relationships, you need to listen and listen and then listen some more. Just because you're not talking doesn't mean you're actually listening. You have to be there and aware.

Try practicing this next time you're in a conversation: Let the other person talk. And then let them talk some more. And then, let them talk even more. You'll be amazed how much information you walk away with. And don't worry that you didn't get to say everything you felt you needed to at the time. You can always schedule a networking meeting with yourself…and do all the talking.

Why I don't talk about *The Price is Right* at networking events.

You know what I want to talk about when I go to a networking event? *The Price is Right*. I love *The Price is Right*! Nothing makes a workout go faster than running on the treadmill during Showcase Showdown. So at events, I'd love to talk about the Cliffhanger challenge and how if you pick $22, $33, and $44 respectively, chances are pretty good you'll win. Did you see that episode where Drew Carey scared the bejesus out of a woman when he yelled *That's too much!* right in her face? I hate to laugh at someone else's expense, but it was really funny. In fact, it was just as funny the tenth time I rewound it and watched it as it was the first time.

You want to know how to make a quick $100,000? Just go on *The Price is Right*, and be picked to play Pay the Rent. Pay the Rent is a game board in the shape of a house with four stories and six grocery items. You need to place the six items in the house in such a way that the sum of the prices of the items on each story is greater than the sum of the prices of the items on the story directly below. You place one item in the mailbox on the first floor, two on the second floor (the stove and the couch), two on the third floor (TV and tub), and one in the safe in the attic.

The key here is the order. You see, most people pick the lowest priced item as the one that goes in the mailbox on the first floor. But that's wrong. You need to pick the fourth lowest priced item as the one for the mailbox. Then, for Floor 2—pick 2 and 3; Floor 3—1 and 5, then put the most expensive items in the attic. And that's how you win $100,000!!

I am a *TPIR* fanatic. But do I talk about this at networking functions? Only in my dreams. You see, I'm no fool. I know the company I'm keeping with my zeal for *The Price Is Right*. The next time I walk into an event surrounded by people on Hoverounds, I know I'm safe to share my *TPIR* wisdom. As far as I can recall, though, I've never seen anyone stroll into a networking event on a Hoveround or talk about a coveted walk-in bathtub. So, at networking functions? Let's just say I'm pretty silent about my love for *The Price is Right*.

Then what do I talk about if not *The Price is Right*? I talk about whatever the other people there want to talk about. The reason I'm there is to get to know other people, not wax eloquent all about me. If that means they want to talk about sports or some other television show, I'm all for it. If they want to tell me what's going on at their company, I'd love to hear it. If they want to share their life story, great, tell me more.

The problem with most people is that they go to a function and immediately start spilling their guts. It's the proverbial showing up and throwing up their life story onto everyone who will listen. I'm okay with it if I'm the one asking the questions. The problem lies with those who aren't prompted for this information.

If you want to be halfway decent at networking and creating great relationships, you need to learn to keep your trap shut. Ask the questions; let others answer. Guide the conversation; don't monopolize it. Figure out what's important to the person across from you and get them to talk about it. Find the fantastic in everyone you meet. It's amazing how a good conversation can lead to a great one.

But if you ever see me at a networking function and want to talk about *The Price is Right*, well, then, *Come on down!*

Structured events

If you're attending a structured sit-down event like a dinner, lunch, or breakfast meeting, the object of the game is to get as many people involved in the conversation as possible. Therefore, be prepared with good table conversation. Scan the newspaper and local business paper so you're up to date on current events. Read *Fortune* magazine, which has great articles about many different industries. Whether you're into entertainment or not, realize that many others are, and it's great content for conversation. *People* magazine and *Us Weekly* let you know who's with whom, who's not, and the latest in the celebrity world.

What about sports? Any big tournaments or events happening? This is a rhetorical question, of course, because there is always some event that just happened or is about to happen. On the next page is a quick reference list of some major sporting and entertainment events and conferences.

Major Sporting/Entertainment Events

January	College Football Bowl Games (Major Bowls), College National Championship, NFL playoffs, NFL Pro Bowl, Australian Open Tennis Tournament; Golden Globes Award Show, Oscar Nominations, Consumer Electronics Show
February	Super Bowl, Winter Olympics (every 4 years), the Oscars, New TV shows debut
March	College Basketball March Madness Tournament, NIT Tournament, Major League Baseball Spring Training, the GRAMMY Awards
April	MLB Opening Day, NFL Draft, NBA Playoffs, the Master's Golf Tournament
May	NBA Championship, French Open Tennis Tournament, Kentucky Derby Horse Race, Preakness Horse Race (2nd leg of the Triple Crown)
June	U.S. Open Golf Tournament, NHL Stanley Cup Finals, Wimbledon Tennis Tournament, World Cup Soccer (every 4 years), Tour de France Cycling Championship, Belmont Stakes (last leg of the Triple Crown), Internet of Things Conference
July	MLB All Star Game, Summer Olympics (every 4 years)
August	NFL Preseason, College Football Season begins, U.S. Open Tennis Tournament
September	MLB Playoffs, Ryder Cup Golf Tournament, New TV shows debut
October	NHL Season Opener, MLB World Series
November	NBA Season Opener, Elections
December	College Football Bowl Games (Minor Bowls), NFL end of regular season

NFL – National Football League   MLB – Major League Baseball
NBA – National Basketball Association   NHL – National Hockey League

This is not an all-inclusive list, but in my experience these are the major events that generally spark conversation at networking events and have the ability to easily include more people in the discussion.

While you may not be a huge fan of television or of sports, again, remember that a lot of people are. If you haven't tuned in at least once to some of the top shows, you should. Because it's not about you talking about your favorites, it's about you asking smart questions. Not sure what's popular? Ask a few friends what they watch, or check out *Us Weekly*. See, it's coming in handier and handier.

I was running a seminar recently when a man seated in the back of the room with his arms crossed and obviously not buying into this concept said, *I would never read* People *magazine, and I don't believe it could help me in any way.* Okay. You're right. Maybe *People* magazine won't help you. But maybe it's not just about *People* magazine. Maybe your attitude won't help you either.

Apparently, all this man wanted to do was talk about golf. That's fine if everyone he meets wants to talk about golf. But he's forgetting the Golden Rule of Networking: *Networking is not about you.* It's about them. It's not about what you're interested in. It's about what they're interested in. If you want to spend the rest of your life only talking about your interests, you're going to have a tough time building a diverse and effective network.

Where do you sit?

If you're attending a sit-down event, you want to be strategic about where you sit in that you want to maximize your time there. Never sit at a table that is empty or partially empty. It might end up staying that way, and you'll find yourself eating alone. Always sit at a table that is almost full—preferably with only one seat left. If two seats are left and they're next to each other, find a different table. That other empty seat might never get taken, and you won't maximize your opportunity to meet people. If two seats are left and they're across the table from each other, feel free to sit at that table.

Once you're seated, if feasible, try to introduce yourself to each person at the table. If there's no conversation going, you may want to get it started with some broad questions about something current. And you know what's current, because you've done your homework.

One time I was speaking at an event where I talked about strategic seating. Come lunchtime, it caused a real problem because nobody wanted to sit down first. You had a bunch of people with full plates from the buffet milling about waiting to see which table would be taken first. At least they'd been listening!

3.2

Sometimes you get stuck. If you have to improvise, be ready to do so. I once went to a breakfast meeting where the entire table conversation was dominated by two people talking about their hometown. I was stuck in the middle of an ad hoc reunion that clearly wasn't ending any time soon. Even if I offered to switch seats, what if they said *No, that's okay*? Then I would really have been stuck. Looking back, I should have moved to a new table. They didn't really care if I was there anyway, and I wasn't able to build any relationships with anyone else at the table because these people were on either side of me.

This experience taught me a lesson. I vowed to never get stuck at the wrong table again. At the very next event, I approached an almost full table and asked, *Are you the fun table?* When the people there said *Absolutely*, I sat down and had one of the most enjoyable networking meals ever, and still keep in touch with a few of the attendees I met.

About the speaker

If you're attending an event with a speaker, you'll often find a crowd around them immediately afterward. If this is someone you want to meet, don't approach on your own, because anyone can do that. Instead, find someone who knows the speaker personally. Perhaps ask around the table where you were sitting or find one of the hosts of the event and ask for an introduction. Then you can approach the speaker and let that person "introduce you." Your credibility is enhanced instantly on the basis of this informal referral. I figured this out when a good friend wanted me to meet Dick Vermeil, former head coach of the Philadelphia Eagles, St. Louis Rams, and Kansas City Chiefs professional football teams. While everyone in front of me was crowding around and gushing about what a great guy he was and asking for his autograph, I had my own personal fan gushing about me to Dick Vermeil. Instead of feeling awkward about having to speak first, I was able to observe, collect some thoughts, and strategize about how to have a conversation that would help me stand out from the rest of his raving fans.

If there's no introduction in sight and you have the opportunity to be the first person in line to meet the speaker, you're in luck. In this situation, you might say, *Hey, you were fantastic. I know a lot of people here want to meet you, so I don't want to take up your time right now. Let me grab your card and I'll follow up with you to schedule a time.*

If you do approach the speaker, don't simply hand over your card and regale them with lines about how great you think they are. That kind of opening can be a little awkward and curtails ongoing conversation. Instead, compliment the speaker and then immediately ask a question to engage them in relevant conversation, maybe something you would have asked that person had they been on a panel. Be sure not to have a long, drawn-out intro to your question. Always ask the question first, and add any commentary after. This gives the person time to think about the answer. The key is to stimulate conversation, not end it. This assumes that you want to build a relationship with the speaker. If you don't, then there's no need to introduce yourself in the first place.

Unstructured events

Unstructured events are typically happy hours or social functions that take place in the evening. If you're not comfortable walking into a party after it's in full swing, then you might want to get there early. Even if you are comfortable walking into an event that's already begun, go early anyway.

3.2

I went to an event early once. Trust me, it was purely accidental. Because there was only one other person there, we talked to each other. Guess what the next person who walked in did? Yes, he joined our impromptu group. The next person after that? You guessed it. She joined us, too. They had to. Why? Because we were the party. When you're the one who arrives earliest, you instantly become the nucleus of the party and the party builds around you. Eventually, you'll likely go off and talk to other people, but it sure is easier to do when you've already had success in meeting a few folks right in the beginning.

One of my favorite things to do is stand by the door and welcome everyone who comes in. *Hello! Great to see you! So glad you could make it.* They remember me for two reasons. First, it's a welcome change at the entrance—to be met by someone who's glad to see you. Second, they often think I'm the host running the event. This combination provides just a little more incentive to remember me.

Why is it important for people to remember you? You're trying to build the foundation for a relationship. It's hard to do that when no one remembers who you are.

The greeting

Most people don't remember names or faces. Most people don't remember all the people they've ever met in their life. Neither do I. Here's my fail-safe way to greet people so I minimize the risk of embarrassing myself:

- If we're meeting for the first time and I know we haven't met before, I say: *Hi, John. I'm Molly Wendell. Nice to meet you.*
- If we see each other and I know for certain we've met before, I say *Hi, John. Molly Wendell. Nice to see you again.*
- If I can't remember whether we've met before or not, I say *Hi, John. Molly Wendell. Nice to see you.*

Nice to meet you. Nice to see you again. Nice to see you.

These three phrases will simplify your life and save you from potential embarrassment. It's funny. Sometimes people don't even listen. When I ran into a woman I couldn't remember meeting before, I brought out the *Nice to see you* line. The woman replied, very enthusiastically, *Molly, I can't believe you remembered me!* And I'm thinking, *Well, I didn't. That's why I said, Nice to see you.* People hear what they want to hear. It's nice when it works in your favor.

What if I've met someone before and they don't remember me?

First, get over yourself. Most people probably won't remember you. Then, adopt the strategy to always introduce yourself with your first and last name. Even if you've met them before, go ahead and say:

Hi, Bill, I'm Tom Smith. We met at [location]. Great to see you again!

Most people are not good at remembering names, yet are offended when others don't remember theirs. Like I said, get over yourself. Once you're certain they know who you are—and you're certain because they said your name before you said theirs—then it's safe to quit with the first/last name greeting. Until then, keep doing it. By the way, if you have a new person join your organization, every time you see them, you should introduce yourself with your first/last name. Not only will you make them feel more comfortable, but they'll likely remember your name before anyone else's.

If you can do something to make it easier for the other person, you should. When I can't remember someone's name, it's easy just to tell them up front. *I'm really sorry. What's your name again?* Other times, I bring someone else into the group and introduce them. For example, let's say I bring Jamie into the group. I'll say—to the person whose name I can't remember—*Have you met Jamie Glass?* and then hope Jamie will say something like *I'm sorry, I didn't catch your name.* Fortunately for me, she usually does.

My husband and I use that same code when we go to parties. Instead of being mad at him afterward for not introducing me, I just assume he can't remember the person's name and I say, *I'm sorry. I didn't catch your name.* It's easy and it works.

What if you've already met someone a few times and he still doesn't remember you? That's right. Get over yourself. I once met a man five times before he finally remembered who I was. I didn't go into too much detail about how we met. Instead, the fifth time, I said, *You know, I think we may have met before at an event back in September, and then many, many years ago when you were with that technology company. It's really great to see you again!* Did it bother me? Not really. Apparently, the other four times, I must not have made much of an impression, even though one of the times was a two-hour, one-on-one job interview where I was offered—but declined—the position. So what? Does he know who I am now? Absolutely.

How to approach a group

Most people I see approaching a group at a networking function do it all wrong. They join a group, interrupt by introducing themselves, and immediately hijack the conversation. It only takes a few minutes before people from the group start leaving.

The easiest way to approach a larger group of people you haven't met is to simply approach and quietly ask one person, *May I join you?* Then politely listen in on the conversation. If and when it's appropriate for you to contribute, you may, but be sure not to steal the floor. Remember, you're a guest to the group. Wait your turn.

If it's just two people, feel free to go up to them, wait for an opening, and say, *I don't believe we've met. I'm Susan Connors.* Then add something like, *I'm sorry. I interrupted. What were you discussing?* You don't want the conversation to end just as you get there. You want it to flow smoothly, and you want to integrate yourself into it. You obviously never want to interrupt someone who's talking either, so be patient waiting for that opening.

The good networker is always prepared to ask great questions to get others talking. Remember what Dale Carnegie said. The more people talk about themselves, the more they like you. You're asking questions to gauge interests and determine if this person might be a good connection for you. Good networkers control conversations by asking questions, but they don't do it in a way that feels like an interrogation. In a controlled environment like this book, practicing and talking about making conversation feels contrived. But when you're with people, interacting, it will likely flow more smoothly. No doubt, it takes practice. But the more you practice, the easier and more natural it becomes.

Are your networking efforts as effective as you think?

I once struck up a conversation at an event with a man I'll call Mike. When I asked Mike what he did, he told me he worked for a bank. A bank I'd never heard of. Coming from Arizona—the land of the bank a minute—I'm used to being exposed to new banks. At least I thought it was new. I asked a bit about his bank. *How long have you been around? Where are you based? How big is it? Who is your target market?* Based on the way Mike was replying, it seemed as if I should have known this information. Apparently, the bank was larger than I'd thought. I was so amazed that this massive bank was not well known, or at least known to me, that I kept asking questions about it.

Mike's tone started to change. He seemed irritated that he was put on the spot to answer questions about his firm. Now, that might be okay if I were some telemarketer interrupting his dinner or something, but we were at a networking event. Isn't the whole point of a networking event to get to know other people, their organizations, and what they do? If Mike didn't want to answer questions about his firm, he probably should've stayed home. If Mike wanted to increase the reputation of his firm, he definitely should've stayed home. Remember, how you show up anywhere is how you show up everywhere.

And that leads me to a fundamental question: *Are your networking efforts as effective as you think?* Certainly many people are attempting to build relationships, but one way or another, they're making a mess of it. Maybe it's glancing at your watch, checking your cell phone, essentially giving off the vibe that says you don't really want to be there. It could be starting your conversation with *Hello, here's my card. Who are you?* And sometimes, it's having a conversation with someone and then, after seeing another person across the room, you stop mid-sentence and say, *Oh, there's Joe. I need to catch up with him.* And off you go.

It's not always what you say. It's how you act. Actions speak louder than words. If your actions are telling other people they're not important, that's a problem. Because at the end of the day, people do business with, or refer business to, people they like. If at the end of the conversation, or even in the middle of it, you're not getting put into the *I really like this person* category, then it might be time to adopt some new approaches. Like what, you ask? How about these: *pay attention, be there and aware*, and *be interesting by being interested*.

The 7 questions that make networking easier and more effective

I'm a big proponent of not waiting for the conversation, but creating the conversation. Starting a conversation effectively is really quite simple. Ask questions. Your questions need to engage people and ensure they spark conversations.

Here's what makes a question great: It needs to give you something to work with, whether it's an opportunity to dig deeper, identify some common ground, find a connection or define, create, or generate a follow-up activity.

When I was in IBM Sales School, we had mock sales calls. I was always graded very poorly on those for not being a good listener. I kept thinking, I heard what you said, but you're grading me on asking 10 questions and I only have 15 minutes in which to ask them, so I'm going to make sure I get those 10 questions in regardless of how you reply. I should have gone with my gut, focused on the responses, worried less about the grade and more about the relationship.

3.2

Well, no one is grading me anymore, and I can ask as few or as many questions as I'd like. Every event I go to, every person I meet, I ask the same questions. Every time. This consistency makes it easy for me to remember the questions. The questions may be the same, but the answers are always different, which enables the conversations to take many different turns.

DON'T WAIT for the conversation. CREATE the conversation.

Here are my 7 questions:

1. *What do you do?*

2. *Where do you work?*

3. *How long have you been there?*

4. *Where were you before that?*

5. *And how long were you there?*

6. *Where were you before that?*

7. *And how long were you there?*

You'll notice that I really only have three questions, because I repeat questions 2 and 3 two times each. Here it is in action:

Hello, I'm Molly Wendell.

Nice to meet you, Molly. I'm Bill Smith.

Great to meet you. So, Bill, what do you do? [Question 1]

I'm in information technology.

That's great. Where do you work? [Question 2]

I work for Banner Health.

What a growing company! How long have you been there? [Question 3]

Two months.

Oh, where you before? [Question 4]

I worked for the Mayo Clinic.

Wow, how long were there? [Question 5]

Just about two years.

Interesting. What were you doing before Mayo? [Question 6]

I was with IBM for 20 years.

Sounds like you must be from Rochester, Minnesota.

Actually I am.

I spent some time in Minnesota [common ground] *and had a lot of friends over at Mayo and IBM. Seems like an interesting transition. What compelled you to join Mayo after being with IBM for so long?* [Notice that I'm moving the conversation back to him.]

Mayo wanted to integrate some new technology that I specialize in.

Interesting, my background is technology, too [common ground]. *What kind of technology?* [Again, moving the conversation back to him.]

3.2

You get the picture. Notice that even though I had the connection of Minnesota, I didn't hijack the conversation and start talking all about myself, but kept the conversation on Bill.

Maybe you haven't spent time in Minnesota, and maybe you're not in technology, but perhaps you know someone who works at Mayo or IBM. Even though they're big companies, you never know if they might know each other.

Let's try another one:

Hello, I'm Karen Niparko.

Nice to meet you, Karen. I'm Jan Dovers.

Jan, what do you do?

I'm an executive recruiter.

Terrific. How long have you been a recruiter?

Actually, just a few years. Before this I worked in human resources for JP Morgan Chase.

Interesting, I work in human resources [common ground]. So, why did you make the switch?

Well, I used to do a lot of high-level recruiting for the new branches we opened, and decided that it was my favorite part of the job. When Executives Network approached me about joining them, I thought it was an easy decision.

That's great! What are you working on these days?

Remember, very few people work for the same organization for their entire career. Very few people are performing the same role in which they got their degree or were initially trained. Very few people live in the same place they were born. And even if they're living in the same region, chances are good that they moved somewhere else for a while.

You may think that these conversations are not particularly fascinating, but you have to start somewhere. Going too deep too quickly runs of risk of alienating someone. I'm not saying you can't

159

get personal, because ultimately that's your goal, to have a personal relationship with the people you want to. At this point, though, you're just trying to build the foundation of a relationship.

The 5 worst conversation starters

How's business? This is bad because only two possible answers exist and both stop the conversation. *Not great, and that's why I'm here at this function, trying to network and build my business.* And this is where the conversation stops. The other answer is *Great.* And this is where the conversation stops.

How about that weather? It's common knowledge that when someone brings up the topic of the weather, it's a sign of boredom. At this point, you may be better served to excuse yourself and find someone interesting, or become more interesting yourself.

3.2

Sometimes questions are just too personal to ask and are not the best to open a conversation.

Are you married?

No.

Do you have kids?

No.

What about pets?

No.

Three strikes. You're out.

People don't realize what land mines these questions are. You really have no idea what their mental state is., and your first encounter with them is probably not the best time to find out.

Before I forget, here's a bonus land mine: *When are you due?* That one has made more than a few of us uncomfortable—both on the giving and receiving end of the question.

Be on the safe side and steer clear of these questions. The only time it is appropriate to discuss topics like these is when the other person brings them up first, such as:

> *I have to leave early and pick up my son from football practice.*
>
> *Oh, how old is your son?*
>
> *I have two. This one is 12.*
>
> *What about the other? Is he a football player as well?*

You get the idea….

Networking Tip:
Remember, it's not about you!

3.2

I am at a networking event and someone from Google is there. Whenever folks from Google are at an event, the line for people wanting to meet them is pretty long. As I'm listening in to hear what people are asking Google Guy, my friend Chris Pelley approaches. Chris starts immediately with the question, *How many of these parents in the room have asked you about getting their son or daughter a job at Google?* Google Guy replies, *Pretty much all of them.* At that point, Chris asks him if he has any kids. Google Guy has a couple, including a daughter just graduating from college. That's when Chris pulls a quite brilliant move. *Well, then, how can I help your daughter in her job search post-school? What is she interested in?*

All of a sudden Chris is on a completely different playing field from everyone else in the room. He isn't *asking* something of Google Guy. He is *giving* something. Remember this next time someone from a coveted company is in the room. This is a great example of thinking about how you can add value to others.

Don't ruin a networking opportunity by focusing so much on you. Think about what value you can bring to them. Open your network to others. The more you do that, the more you'll find that others open their network to you.

Here's my card. Uhhh, no thanks!

When do we exchange business cards? That depends. As I mentioned before, my take on business cards is that you want to get them, not give them. If you're speaking with someone who seems interesting, and you'd like to set up a time to meet, it's time to say, *I'd love to talk more about this. Let me get your card and I'll follow up with you.* Do you give your card to that individual? Not unless they ask for it.

I was in a taxi and the driver was sharing some incredible insight he read in a networking book, which recommended giving your business card to everyone you meet and telling them if there's any way you can help them, they should give you a call. I find so much wrong with this concept that I almost don't know where to begin.

First, if I meet you and you immediately hand me your card, I've got news for you: I don't know whether your card deserves to take up real estate in my purse. And as all women know, that's some of the most valuable real estate around. I can't have it cluttered with a bunch of cards of people I don't care to know. What I'm saying is, please don't hand me your card until you've earned the right, and by earning the right, I mean because I specifically asked for your card.

Second, it's not my job to figure out how you can help me. That's your job. If you can't figure out how to help me, then I'm not sure you can help me. That's like going to the doctor and saying your back hurts and having the doctor give you a card and tell you to schedule another appointment once you've figured out exactly how to fix it. Who'd go back to that doctor?

You might be thinking, *Why would I want to figure out how to help you?* Well, right back at you. Perhaps that's what relationships are all about. Thinking about others and identifying ways to help them is what makes you a great networker.

Quit thinking that the more cards you hand out, the better you are at networking. Better yet, forget about giving your card out at all. Focus more on earning the right to take the relationship to another level by figuring out how to help someone, and then act on it. The smart ones will most certainly ask for your card.

What if someone has a lead for me? Should I give my card then? Maybe. If someone has a lead or contact for you, you should say, *Great, do you have a card?* Get theirs and then you can control the communication.

I met a woman who told me about a great lead she got from the person next to her on an airplane. *I hope he calls me,* she said. She'd given him her card, but hadn't gotten any contact information from him. He was out of cards. Which goes back to what I said about always carrying pen and paper with you. Now, this woman's great lead is at the mercy of someone else's timeframe, memory, and organizational skills. How many times have you lost someone's card or forgotten to follow up? Guess what? They have as well.

What if the conversation gets stuck?

You're at a networking function talking with one person. The conversation is not really going anywhere. What do you do? If you decide you need to move on, I'll share a couple of things to do. But first, I'll share what not to do.

DON'T say to the person, *Nice talking to you.* Or, *Well, you're here to meet people and I am, too. Thanks for your time.* Or, *I have to go to the restroom.* And then leave them standing alone. Nothing is worse than being left all alone at a networking function. Nothing cries out Inconsiderate Networking Rookie more than the person who leaves someone standing all alone.

DO…one of the following:

1. Wait until someone joins your group, make the introduction, and then, while they're engaged in conversation, quietly excuse yourself.

2. Find someone to join your group (preferably someone standing all alone), make the introduction, and give the new person some context, such as *Bill, we were just talking about…*. Then, while they're engaged in conversation, quietly excuse yourself.

3. If no one else is around, then you'll need to get a little creative. Say something like:

   I'm hungry. Do you want to get something from the buffet?

   Come on, let's go meet some more people.

   Offer to bring them with you to meet others. If they leave you at that point, fine. But never leave someone else standing alone.

What's a success?

I was headed to a conference in France. Was it going to result in some business? I had no idea. But one thing I did know was that if I didn't go, I definitely wouldn't get any business out of it. Sometimes you have to throw caution to the wind, and pray for the best.

I get in touch with my friend Emilie Meinadier, whom I'd met a few years back on a yoga retreat in India. Emilie works in the fashion business. Fortunately, my trip coincides with the tail end of Paris Fashion Week, which means she'll be available to get together.

It turns out that Emilie has recently experienced some significant life changes and is trying to figure out how to redefine herself for the future. Whether it's identifying new trends for a fashion magazine or connecting a hot, new designer with a major retailer, when Americans in the fashion world come to Paris, the smart ones work with Emilie. Emilie is completely connected, and she knows how to get things done. We talk about a potential opportunity to bring some U.S. executives to Paris to meet with fashion executives. Her challenge, she says, is that the U.S. executives expect her to fill the room. In other words, quantity over quality. We talk about how to reset and redefine those expectations. *I mean, really,* I say, *If the U.S. team goes back to the States with five great designers in their back pocket, wouldn't that be a coup?* Emilie says yes. *And if they go back with three, what about then? Well,* Emilie says, *that'd be good, too. What if they go back with two, but the two are amazing designers? Well,* Emilie says, *that'd work. So, what if they go back with only one, one single designer, but it is the best one ever, the one who can redefine a marketplace? Wouldn't that be one more than they had before their trip? Well,* Emilie says, *yes, yes, it would.*

3.2

165

So really, it's not about quantity. Well, it is, but in this case, the quantity is one. It's more about redefining expectations of what you're trying to accomplish. Most people are focused on quantity because they've never had quality. Oftentimes, because most people are not prepared to handle it, when you produce too much quality opportunity or activity, many of those opportunities get lost.

The bottom line: If you can get one good contact at any event, consider it a success.

Again, what's your goal?

Get out there. Bring that "A" game. Engage in interesting, meaningful conversation. Make new friends. Stop allowing the conversations to go on without you. But don't ever lose sight of your primary goal when meeting new people: to ask yourself the question, *How can I help them?* and not the other way around. Use smart, relevant questioning to figure it out. At the end of the day, it's simply about being a good, helpful person. That's what you're trying to do. It reminds me of my sister Betsy's favorite t-shirt that says BE*lieve* THE*re is* GOOD *in the world*. Notice the bolded letters: BE THE GOOD. Think about that. Be the good.

The Networked Organization Action Plan

- It's not about you. It's about them.
  Ask questions to get them talking.

- Don't give cards; get cards.

- It only takes one good contact to make
  a networking event a success.

- Be the good. Figure out how you can help others.

3.2

3.3

NETWORKING AT 30,000 FEET

Networking doesn't only happen at formal networking events. The opportunity to network is all around you; it's up to you to be ready for it. It will probably come as no surprise by now that one of my

favorite places to network is on an airplane. I enjoy it because not only do I get to travel to new, exciting places, but I get to meet new, exciting people I may not have an opportunity to meet otherwise. It's also worth mentioning that I've gotten more business from the people who sit next to me on flights than any other source.

If you don't ever **LEAVE** your house, you likely won't meet **ANYONE** you don't already **KNOW.**

Have you ever seen the comedian Louis C. K. talk about the miracle of flying in an airplane? Most people complain, he says, when they should be amazed that they're flying through the air, sitting in a chair…in the sky! Most people would rather whine about how bad the lines are at airport security, how inconvenient the 30-minute delay is going to be, how stale the food is, if there is any. If there isn't, they complain about the lack of food.

But if you're going to travel, you need to approach travel like an attraction, not an obligation. You need to be ready to meet new people and believe you'll have great conversations on the flight. You need to know that this flight is not just taking you to where you need to be, but taking you on a journey toward a potential new relationship.

Networking opportunities: They're everywhere.

3.3

This particular trip takes me to Bali, Indonesia, and Sydney, Australia. Because my husband and I have different airline allegiances, I sometimes find myself meeting him at our destination, as is the case on this trip. When you travel alone, the opportunity to meet really interesting people can be so much greater than when traveling with friends or family. Do you have any idea how many people you can meet on any given trip? Let me give you a little glimpse.

The first person I meet is at the United Club Lounge at Los Angeles International Airport. We are both headed to the coffee machine. But this is no ordinary coffee machine. This one looks like you need a Masters of Barista Science from Starbucks University in order to figure out how to work it. As we are discussing whether either of us has such training (the answer is a resounding no), we take the opportunity to find out what each other does. He works for the President. Yes, the President of the United States. How cool is that? You can be sure I get his card.

Then, on my flight, I meet a woman who lives in Australia and has been to Bali many times. She gives me all kinds of great ideas about places to go and things to do. Plus, she has the inside scoop on our seats, which, according to her, are too close to the cockpit and very noisy. We have the option to move to some other seats and she volunteers us. I am lucky to have met her.

On the train from the airport into central Sydney, I meet a woman who works for the Tourist Board of New South Wales who is nice enough to courier over some great tourist information to our hotel.

In Bali, we take the Banyan Bike Tour of the rice paddies, a must-do if you're ever in Bali. We meet a photographer based in Australia (who could use the NSW Tourist Board contact?) and his wife, who works for a charity based in Colorado near where we live. Then we meet some other people who are moving to Portland, one who is going to work for a big advertising agency that works with Nike. I am planning to be in Portland in a few months, and it will be good to reconnect.

On the way home, I sit next to a really interesting man who runs Global Risk for a major bank. The conversation is fascinating. Both his birthday and anniversary are coming up, giving me a good reason to follow up with him. Plus, I met someone a couple months earlier who might be a good connection for him.

While waiting for our bags at the pre-customs baggage claim, I meet someone who works for the company that makes Happy Meal toys for McDonald's. He's from Australia, but based in Chicago. In the customs line, it turns out the person behind

3.3

me runs a number of businesses throughout the world, but also used to run a CEO network in Australia and New Zealand. Might be a good person to know.

Finally, on my flight back to Denver, I sit next to someone who manages a coal mine. This is really interesting because a couple weeks ago I met some executives from a mining services company, so I have a little more frame of reference for his business. In fact, he should meet the folks from the mining services company. I'll set that up.

I probably could meet a few more people in the gate area, but my connection from Los Angeles to Denver is really tight and I make it to the gate just in time for boarding.

The point here is that there's opportunity to meet all kinds of people in all kinds of places. You never know who you're going to be standing in front of or behind, seated next to, or hanging out with in the same general area. By the way, while it may seem like it, I'm really not standing around introducing myself to everyone I see. When people are waiting, they're passing time. They're open to the right person striking up a conversation. You have to be that right person. Remember, don't wait for the conversation. Create the conversation. Be on the lookout for an opening. Have a friendly face on. You can't be talking on your phone, emailing someone, or listening to music. You have to be in the moment, completely aware of your surroundings and the opportunities they present. Trust me, these opportunities will present themselves to you time and time again. It's time to start paying attention.

Do you have any idea how fascinating people are?

I went to a funeral a few years back. My friend's mom had passed away. My memory of her mom was pretty distinct. She was a very nice woman who wore a flowered apron, cleaned the house a lot, and always managed to be taking cookies out of the oven when we arrived. Talk about some good timing! My friend's mother was dainty. Frail. Pleasant. Likely not someone who would ruffle too many feathers. Definitely not someone I would consider a risk taker.

During the funeral, they talked about her life. It turns out, aside from her incredibly honed skill as a baker, this woman had another life that I, and many others in the room, had known nothing about. During World War II, she'd been part of the Underground, transporting weapons. Yes, our very own Mrs. Cleaver used to fill her bicycle basket with machine guns, put a blanket over them, and ride past enemy checkpoints to deliver them to the Allies.

If only I'd known. If only I'd known what a truly fascinating woman she was. But I had no idea. I simply assumed that she'd been into cleaning and cookies all her life. I really missed out on this one. I missed out on the opportunity to talk to this strong and fearless woman; to find out what drove her to do what she did. To hear the stories. What compelled her to risk her life? What other daring escapades had she undergone?

Now, I'll never know. Now, it's too late.

This situation taught me something very important. Everyone has something interesting to share. Everyone has done something fascinating. Everyone has things they've accomplished, people they've met, or experiences they've had that make them what they are today. It's my job to find the fascinating. Now, it's your job too.

173

I'm on an airplane in a window seat, which is not my preference. The middle seat is open, but not for long, as a large man is walking down the aisle heading toward my row. He squeezes into the middle seat right next to me. This could be a really uncomfortable flight. Then again, it could be one of the best flights of my life. It's my choice. Right here. Right now.

I decide to make it the best flight of my life. I introduce myself to my new seatmate. I mean, if we're going to share a seat, the least we can do is know each other's names, right? Soon, I'm asking Mike questions about what he does. The conversation takes some turns, as they tend to do. Next thing you know, I come to find out that Mike's first job was definitely out of the ordinary. He says the hardest call he's ever made was telling his parents that he'd just graduated from college and landed a job. As a professional black jack cheater. Wow!

3.3

Hours seem like mere minutes as we talk through the entire flight. And you know what? I could have judged him. I could have decided that he wasn't interesting at all. I could have decided not to engage in conversation. Here's what happens instead. I learn some really interesting things about casino operations. I hear a lot of great stories. I have a great time. And I make a new friend.

You know how cats have nine lives. Well, so do people. If I look back at who I've been over my lifetime, I've definitely morphed myself a few times over the course of adulthood. Someone who meets me today will see me as a very different person from someone who met me years ago, when I was still pulling consecutive all-nighters working for IBM. I'm not sure which life I'm on right now, but I know I have plenty more to come. And so do you.

I remind myself of this every time I meet someone. I always assume that everyone is fascinating, with a fascinating mind, a fascinating past, and a fascinating future. My mission is to figure out what's so very fascinating about them. And you should make it your mission, too. With this attitude, you'll be amazed what different conversations you have with people, and how you can build deeper and more meaningful relationships. Do it quickly, though. Because it's really hard to build a relationship with people when you're listening to their eulogy.

How do you connect at 30,000 feet?

Mastering the art of conversation is one thing. Mastering it on the airplane is another. As I've mentioned, you have to be there and aware. You also have to be strategic about how you pick your moments.

Before you board

3.3

When booking a flight, go for the exit row. Premium flyers take the exit row. Given they travel a lot, they're more likely to know more people around the globe. This is not to say that I haven't met some very interesting people seated elsewhere on the plane, but given the choice, I'll take exit row over a regular economy seat.

If I have the choice of upgrading to first class a few days before the flight, I always take a seat next to one that is already taken. Either that person paid for a first-class ticket, or their status enabled them to be upgraded early. It gives me some indicator that either they, or their company, can afford to pay for first class and maybe I want to do business with them, or they fly frequently and are well-traveled—which always makes for interesting conversation for me.

In the security line and the boarding area, pay attention for opportunities to strike up a conversation.

My friend Susan once told me about a trip she and her business partner took. Susan saw someone wearing a shirt with a corporate logo on it. She wanted to meet someone from that firm, so she struck up a conversation. She ended the conversation by taking the person's business card with a promise for a follow-up call. When she sat down, her business partner looked at her strangely and said, *What are you doing?* Her reply: *I'm channeling Molly.*

Sometimes that's just it. Sometimes you just have to *channel Molly*. Take yourself out of your comfort zone and have the attitude that an opportunity may be right within your reach. Grab it!

Take your seat.

Once you're situated, it's time to pull out your stuff. All of it. You need to look like you have a lot you plan to accomplish during this flight. Sometimes this is a decoy. Sometimes it's a life preserver. Based on the flight time, bring out the file folders, magazines, books/kindles, iPads, computers; whatever it takes that says *I've got a lot going on and I plan to get a lot done on this flight.* The last person you want to be seated next to is the person who has nothing to do…for the next three hours.

One of the most important things is to start the conversation sometime after the airplane door shuts and prior to takeoff. This ensures that you're not interrupting an important last-minute phone call and that the conversation will begin before they tune you out with their headphones.

How do you get things going?

First, you want to know who the person is who's sitting next to you. I always start my airplane conversations with the same line I used when I met James Caan: *Are you coming or going? Are you going home or going away?*

Which always leads to my next question: *And what brings you to (or what brought you to) [city]?*

If they say business, say, *What kind of business are you in?*

If they name an industry, but don't mention the company, ask which company. Then, ask what they do for the company and how long they've been there. And, where were they before that? And how long were they there? And where before that? If these questions sound familiar, it's because they are the same ones you use at a networking event. Keep it simple. Make it easier for you to get the conversation started.

Next, come back to what's going on in this person's world today. If you know a few players in the industry, say, *Do you compete with [company]?* If you're unsure where they fit in the market, ask who their competitors are.

Your goal? To gain an understanding of what's going on in that industry. Ask something like *What's the latest and greatest in [industry]?*

This is usually plenty to get people started. In fact, the question about what they do is usually enough.

Then, sit back, listen, and enjoy the ride. Listen for opportunities to ask more questions. Listen for opportunities to ask for clarification. Listen for opportunities to create value through an idea, lead, or contact, giving you a reason to follow up.

I like a follow-up plan, but without some action item buried in the conversation, the follow up has less meaning. I often write down some action items on a separate piece of paper—other than on the contact's card—because I want to capture it right away. I rarely get someone's contact information/business card until the end of the flight, usually when we're about to deplane, and if I waited until then to capture my follow up, it will probably be long forgotten.

What is considered too much information (TMI)…really?

When you use this approach of questioning, you'll find that people tend to talk. A lot. Once I was on a flight employing my casual questioning line when the man sitting next to me actually said, *I feel like there should be a spotlight on me. When is it my turn to ask you a question?* I laughed. *I'm so sorry. You can ask me anything. But, just real quick, one more question.* Of course, that kept us going the rest of the flight. He didn't really have any pressing questions for me. At this point, a lot of you might say, *What a self-centered person he was to not ask you even one question.* But I'm okay with that. I want people to be, for lack of a better word, self-centered. I want people to be okay with telling me all about themselves. I'm okay with TMI. Remember, who do I know better than anyone else? Who do I know the most? That's right. Me. How much more information do I need to know about myself? Not much.

> Who do I know better than anyone else?
>
> # ME.
>
> How much more information do I need to know about myself?
>
> ## NOT MUCH.

It's amazing what people will tell you if you just ask. I took my seat next to a man who was on the phone. His conversation went something like this: *Hi babe. I'm on the plane and we're getting ready to take off. I'll call you when I land, babe. I love you.* He hung up the phone and then made another call. *Hi, babe. I'm on the plane and we're getting ready to take off. I'll call you when I land, babe. Love you.*

After he hung up, I looked at him and said, *You have two babes. Tell me more!* And he did. Near the end of the flight, he told me, *You know more about me than my family does.*

Well, I sure hope so!

Sometimes, continuing the conversation takes precedence over comfort. How many times has my bladder been about to burst, but I've been too deep in conversation to interrupt the flow? Plenty of times! When I can't wait any longer, I say, *Hold that thought, I'll be right back.* It's up to you to remember where that person left off, though, because you'll likely have to remind them what they were talking about.

The majority of my flights end with the people next to me telling me this was the most enjoyable flight they've ever had. This is exactly what Dale Carnegie was trying to get across. The more people talk about themselves, the more they like you. It's tough to nurture a relationship with someone who doesn't like you. So, get them to talk. Get them to like you. That's your first priority.

3.3

Now I know why people don't want to talk on airplanes!

I pride myself on meeting new people on planes and having interesting discussions. But what I witnessed one day has to be the reason so many people are gun shy about striking up conversations on airplanes.

It's a quick flight from Phoenix to Denver, about an hour and a half flight time. I take my aisle seat and notice as a woman (turns out her name is Cathy) across the aisle strikes up a conversation with the person in the window seat next to her. I'm using the word *conversation* loosely here. Very loosely. This goes on for about 20 minutes while the plane is boarding. Yes, she's from the East Coast. No, she wasn't affected by the hurricane that much. Well, she has two kids and a dog, so she was really worried about how they'd handle it. She teaches at a university. She's hoping to get tenure in a few years. She doesn't know, maybe 10? But she really wanted to be a clinician.

Her rant goes on until it's interrupted by a new passenger who takes the middle seat. Oh, the poor soul. He has no idea what he's in for. *Yes, hi, yes, headed to DC. I'm a teacher. I really like it, but I wanted to be a clinician. They make four times the money as we teachers.* Even her graduating students make more money than she does. Not that she's bitter. Well, it's all because of her high-school counselor. Apparently, when he was writing his five-page letter of recommendation, it included some not-so-recommended items.

Cathy sounded something like this [I've inserted my own thoughts in brackets]:

My high school counselor wrote a five-page letter of recommendation. I mean, that's unheard of. [You mean, someone as talkative as you? Yes, simply unheard of.] *They typically write one- to two-page letters, but this guy wrote a glowing five-page letter.* [Yes, you mentioned that.]

But somewhere in the five pages there was one teeny, tiny paragraph sandwiched in between all the good stuff where he said my interpersonal skills were lacking; that I was aloof and wouldn't do well helping people. [Wow, who knew high-school counselors were so astute?] *What do I mean by aloof? Well, standoffish, maybe, but that's not me at all.* [No, I wouldn't call it standoffish either as much as annoying.] *And just because of that, he thought I wouldn't be good interacting with people. Boy, was he wrong.* [No. No, he wasn't.] *I'm great with people.* [No, you're not.]

This woman Cathy goes on and on and on.

In fact, she goes on for so long that I finally try to drown her out. It's very difficult. Chatty Cathy just won't give my ears a break. I mean, she talks nonstop for the entire flight. One and a half hours! I'm sure if the flight went on longer, she'd keep talking. Her monologue is painful for me. As it is, I'm sure, for the guy sitting next to her. Put a lid on it, Cathy!

So, now I understand. I get it. Now I understand why so many people don't want to talk on planes. They must have experienced getting stuck listening non-stop to a *not* bitter, *not* aloof, annoying seatmate.

3.3

Next time you absolutely need to escape, here are a few things you can do:

1. *Get up to use the restroom. When you get back, put your headphones on immediately and don't make eye contact.*
2. *Look at the TV screen and say, I've been wanting to catch this TV show. Put your headphones on.*
3. *Tell the person you're right in the middle of the best part of your book and you need to finish it before the flight lands.*
4. *Tell her you need to do some work, then break out your computer.*
5. *Tell her you need to do some work, then break out your copy of Us Weekly.*
6. *Hold your eyes closed for longer than expected. Then, open them and say, Wow, I must've dozed off. I'm really tired. I think I'm going to take a little nap.*

7. Start coughing uncontrollably. You should be good for the rest of the flight.

The reality is that you really don't owe your seatmate an explanation for not wanting to talk, or listen, to them. If you have any level of human empathy, however, it's best to be armed with some type of excuse that gets you off the hook gently.

Perhaps more to the point: Next time you're on a flight, make sure you're not the one annoying the people around you. If you're doing more than half the talking, you just may be the Chatty Cathy who people want to get away from.

On occasion, I admit I may come off as annoying. I remember the flight when I sat next to a man who was in broadcasting. When I asked him what aspect of broadcasting, he said he was on TV. I asked him which show because he certainly didn't look like anyone I'd ever seen before. Turns out this man was an investigative reporter for a news magazine show like *60 Minutes*, only the other one. He talked for about 15 minutes and then told me he didn't want to talk about himself. No problem, I had plenty to do. About 30 minutes later, I had a thought, and asked him another question. After a 10-minute long answer, he again told me he didn't want to talk about himself. I kept thinking, if you don't want to talk about yourself, then why are you giving me such long, involved answers? For someone who was in the business of ratings and being watched on TV, he sure acted like a paparazzi target dealing with some raving lunatic of a fan. Who did he think he was? Someone really famous?

Yes, I knew he didn't want to talk, mostly because he flat out told me so…twice. And yes, I took that information to heart and left him alone. But it is the rare individual who doesn't enjoy a good conversation about themselves.

Sometimes, I don't want to talk on the flight either. Sometimes it's because I can't hear you, or you have bad breath (typically caused by garlic, onions, or smoking), or you've had too much to drink, or I'm so tired that I need to get some sleep on this particular segment of my trip. This is especially the case for international trips heading east where you'll be a mess when you land if you don't get some sleep during the flight. Keep these things in mind if the person next to you isn't willing to engage. It may or may not be about you.

3.3

The Networked Organization Action Plan

- Networking is about everyone but you. The more you ask, the more you learn.
- Select your seat carefully.
- Find the fascinating in everyone you meet.
- A good networking conversation rarely consists of your doing any of the conversing.
- Avoid drinking alcohol at networking events, including on airplanes.

3.3

Networking at Trade Shows and Conferences

Conferences and trade shows can be very valuable if you approach them strategically. What's great about them is that the people attending have a similar interest in the topic and are there to learn and meet other people. Generally, removing people from their office environment also helps them be a bit more relaxed. If you've made the decision to invest your time and money to attend or sponsor a trade show, let's make sure you're maximizing your efforts and optimizing your return on time and investment.

Exhibiting on the trade show floor

What do you hear when you walk by a booth? *Have you seen what we do? Can I show you a demo? Can I tell you a little bit about our product?* What are you thinking as you hear these statements designed to pull you in? Maybe all you want to do is take a look at the offerings without being pressured, peruse a brochure, or peek over someone's shoulder to see a demo in progress. Sometimes you want the chance to ask questions, but only if you have a genuine interest in learning more. Initial questions of the typical exhibitor are generally centered around their own products and services. In other words, me, me, me.

If you're going to make the considerable investment of time and money to be at the show, you need to focus on how you'll gain enough value to make the investment pay off.

Let's think for a minute. Who's walking by your booth? It could be a prospect, it could be a referral source, it could be someone just looking for the free t-shirt. Whichever type of person it is, there's value in engaging each one of these types to understand more.

And how are we going to do that? While they're waiting in line for the free t-shirt, have your team ready to strike up a conversation. Yes, get them talking about themselves. Get them to like you. If it's a bona fide prospect, they'll naturally have questions around your solution. If they're just there for the free t-shirt, be gracious. You never know who they know and could refer.

Here is what I recommend to people working the booth. First, get the attendees talking in a safe and non-threatening way. Ask the questions you always ask:

- *Where do you work?*
- *How long have you been there?*
- *And where were you before that?*

Then, go into event specific questions like:

- *What compelled you to attend today? What are you especially interested in finding a solution for?* If the answer does not include your solution, think about other vendors at the event to whom you could refer the prospect.

- *What are you finding of most value at the show/conference/event?*
- *What all do you do/what is your scope of responsibility?* If this has been answered by the prior question, there's no need to repeat the question.

Then, as they've started to warm up to you, transition into more business specific questions. Let's assume you sell cybersecurity-related products. Consider using some or all of the following:

- *How is your role impacted by cybersecurity breaches?*
- *How much do you get involved in efforts to prevent cybersecurity breaches?*
- *What we're seeing in the market is that people in your role are most impacted by [fill in the blank] type of breach. What are you seeing?*
- *Can I take a moment to share what we're doing to help prevent security breaches and shorten the time from breach to detection if the bad guys do get through? I'd love to get your insights and see what you think.*
- *For people in your role, we've found that the [XYZ capability] is of great interest. What do you think?*

3.4

As you create your own flow of questions, you'll notice from the above example that the initial objective is to engage the attendees so they are comfortable talking with the booth team. Only after establishing some level of rapport is it appropriate to delve into questions relevant to the domain of your solution. From there the flow can proceed a number of ways, but any good qualification process should focus on leading the customer to your solution through engagement, not by pushing your product on them.

Again, always be gracious to the free t-shirt recipients. You still never know who they know.

Walking the floor

There are as many different reasons people attend trade shows and conferences as there are people who attend them: some are looking for new solutions to a specific problem; some attend training; some want to see what's new in the market; some just want to meet others in similar roles. Often it's a combination of reasons. Walking the show floor with its many booths can therefore be both a valuable and at times overwhelming experience. For this reason, I coach people to walk the floor with a sense of purpose and with their priorities in mind.

For example, if you're attending to learn about a specific solution, you'll likely want to prioritize on those booths and visit them first. Keep in mind that you might not only find a new solution that could benefit your company, but also meet a referral source for new customer opportunities, an influencer or even a new potential employee. Questions I like to ask when coming up to a booth include:

3.4

- *So tell me, what you do at [XYZ company]?*
- *How long have you been at the company?*
- *And where were you before that?*

Sound familiar? Yes, I'm sure they do. Even if you're simply interested in what solution they offer, getting the booth personnel to like you will result in a more valuable conversation than if they simply scan your badge and put you on an email list. They'll know you're interested, engaged, and easy to talk with about what they have to offer. You also might find that the more you engage, the more you'll find out about special offers they only communicate to VIP customers. Or you could be asked to be on an advisory board or council, which are great networking opportunities, by the way.

Next, it's time to progress to more specific questions to learn about their product or solution. Here are a few questions that may at first seem different from what you're used to, but offer great insights into the product:

- *What's a typical customer for you? Size? Revenue? Number of employees? Maybe I know someone I can introduce you to.* Remember to figure out ways to provide value to others.

- *In the market, when you win, why do you win? What problem do you solve?* These questions can help crystalize what is truly different about their product. If it's price alone, what happens when a lower price provider comes into the market?

- *When you lose, why do you lose? Who do you lose to?* Every company loses a deal from time to time. This question gives insight into not only why they lose, but perhaps also into potential limitations of their product that could be important to you. It might also give you ideas about what other companies you ought to look at since those are the ones that win.

It's coffee break time.

Coffee breaks are great opportunities to meet lots of people. Much like scenarios described in other sections of this book, you want to ensure you don't barge into a conversation already in progress. But there are lots of good times to start a conversation. One I like especially is while waiting in line for coffee. Normally, people are just standing there. Always start with these questions so you can begin to identify what their network looks like:

- *Where do you work?*
- *How long have you been there?*
- *And where were you before that?*

A next set of good conversation questions might be:

- *So, what are you finding has been the greatest value for you today?*
- *What have you seen that's new and different?*
- *Of all the events you could have attended, what compelled you to come to this one?*
- *What other events do you attend that you find valuable?*

Each person you meet, each company you are introduced to, is a new opportunity to build a relationship. Engage people in conversation. Understand their business. Figure out who might be good prospects for them. Again, get them to like you.

Sometimes you can engage someone by giving them a mission. *Hey, I'm trying to find someone here who is connected with [ABC Company]. Any ideas?* When faced with the prospect of networking in an open room, most people would rather be put to work.

Parties and special events

Many trade shows and conferences include evening events. Sometimes these are sit-down dinners. You should treat these dinners as you would any typical networking event and follow the information outlined in Section 3.2 on Networking Events.

What about when an event seems more like a party? Companies like to host parties with some entertainment, typically in the form of a very loud band. It's really tough to have a conversation when you're being drowned out by *The Heart of Rock & Roll* by Huey Lewis and The News (didn't they retire a million years ago?). What do you do then? Here's what I'd recommend. Go to the edges. The outskirts, such as the entrance/registration area, where you can greet people. The patio is another good place. Or, if you meet an interesting person in a too-loud area, ask to step outside to continue the conversation without having to be a lip reader.

It may seem obvious, but take it easy on the alcohol. Maybe even avoid it altogether; drink club soda instead. I love a great martini, but not when I'm networking. Why? It's too easy for people to have another, then maybe another. Maybe you can hold your alcohol. Maybe you can't. Now is not the time to find out. You work far too hard building a great reputation to risk damaging it at an event. This very situation happened to someone I know at a December holiday party. Months later people are still talking about the guy who had way too many drinks. Do you really want to be that guy?

And for all of you event planners who continue to believe that attendees everywhere are interested in listening to loud rock bands from their youth who don't sound half as good as they used to, well, they're not. Attendees are there to build new relationships. They'd rather enjoy a venue with good lighting so they can see who they're talking to, soft music so they can hear who they're talking to, and a reasonable ending time so they can get a good night's sleep. Or at least set the expectation that the first 90 minutes are for networking by providing soft background music before turning up the volume for the party that kicks in at 9 PM. Just a thought….

Another thought. Be creative. Maybe offer some kind of team event, a competition where people can meet new people in a structured, but fun way during a unique experience. At one event where I was speaking, one of the activities was a bike-building competition. The hosts divided people into different teams. Each team had to build two children's bikes and then nominate a rider for the bike races to follow. It was hilarious watching the six-foot man pedaling around on a three-foot pink bicycle with ribbons on the handlebars through a course outlined with bicycle boxes. As a bonus, after the event all the bicycles were donated to a charity.

This is a great example of a unique event that included teambuilding, networking, a lot of laughter and philanthropy. Nice job, Stacey Gerber! More events should be like this.

Conferences

Conferences are great ways to meet new people and offer all kinds of opportunities. Many of the techniques mentioned previously are great for conferences. The only material difference between conferences and other events is that at conferences you tend to spend more time sitting, listening to speakers.

Want to maximize your time at the conference? First, make sure to sit in the best seat in the house. What's the best seat in the house? It's the seat along the middle aisle, one quarter to one third of the way up (closer to the back of the room than the front), second seat in. Sit there and you'll be what I like to call the Lucky Seat Winner.

When I was in fourth grade, my Girl Scout troop went to see a live taping of a children's show called *Wallace and Ladmo*. Before the show started, I asked my friend Stacey if I could switch seats with her because I seemed to have lost my glasses and couldn't see anything beyond four feet in front of me. Stacey willingly moved back two rows and I moved forward to take her seat. Prior to the show taping, the producer showed up and asked the audience some questions. Who's watched *Wallace and Ladmo*? A bunch of hands went up. Who has a *Wallace and Ladmo* savings account? Only one hand went up. Mine. Later in the show, they did something with the audience called the Lucky Seat Winner. Wallace told Ladmo to move up one row and move over two seats where, *voilà*, the Lucky Seat Winner would be. Of course it was me. Stacey was so mad!! She thought I'd duped her into moving seats and somehow won the prize. But I knew better. I knew that the Lucky Seat was whichever seat I happened to be sitting in. After all, who else in the audience had a *Wallace and Ladmo* bank account? No one. Who else was there supporting their brand extension beyond watching the show? No one.

Since that day, I've chosen my seat carefully.

Here's why you want a seat along the middle aisle, about one third of the way up, second seat in: Because you'll experience turnover. The seat next to you will likely turn over multiple times within a session. Most people walk into a venue using the back, middle doors. Latecomers only want to go up a few rows before taking a seat. The aisle seat is the preferred seat so they don't have to walk past someone to get to a chair. Latecomers are also typically, but not always, people who are easily interrupted. An important phone call, an email, a text—any distraction will do—to give them reason to get up and leave the room and make room for another latecomer to sit next to you.

The key is to quickly engage your new seatmate once they are seated. *Hey, you haven't missed much. I'm Molly Wendell, by the way. What's your name? Great to meet you.* Get a good look at the individual's name badge. Maybe they'll give you a card. If not, you know who they are. You don't want to interrupt the speaker, but sometimes, really, let's face it, some speakers deserve to be interrupted, at least the ones who shouldn't be speakers in the first place. If your new neighbor makes a motion to get up and leave, say, *Hey, let me grab a card. If they say anything interesting, I'll be sure to let you know.*

3.4

Remember, power people sit on the aisle. If you want to increase your chances of meeting more power players, keep the aisle seat next to you available for them.

The Elevator/Escalator

If you find yourself with a captive audience, leverage it. If the conference/trade show is located in or near the hotel you're staying in, you might find that a great networking opportunity is the elevator. Start off with something like *Are you here for the conference? Me too. What do you do? And how long have you been there?* Think about people you've met that you could connect them to. Give them a reason to want to exchange contact information with you.

I was at a conference recently where I kept meeting really interesting people in the elevator. Sometimes, if we didn't have a chance to exchange cards during the ride, I'd step out when they did. One person said, *Oh, is this your floor? No,* I told him, *we passed my floor long ago.* I started to look for more reasons to ride the elevator, and every time, every single time, I met someone who could be a good contact for me. This happened on the escalator, too. A shorter ride, but we all had the same exit point. Imagine having your employees take turns riding the elevator/escalator all day long (or at least during peak hours). Imagine how many more connections your team could make!

3.4

Trade Show White Thing (TSWT)

Lastly, before we end this section, I must address something I call Trade Show White Thing (TSWT). This is so disgusting I hate to even bring it up. But what's more disgusting is watching it for an extended period of time. Trade Show White Thing is what you get when you're at a trade show and don't drink enough water. TSWT often starts in the corner of your lip and moves from your top lip to your bottom lip every time you bring your lips together. TSWT is typically the combination of too much talking, too much coffee, too little water, and is usually accompanied by very bad breath. TSWT can turn off anyone in mere seconds.

How do you ensure you don't contract TSWT? It's easy. Limit your coffee/tea intake. Drink plenty of water. Keep a glass or bottle of water (and a mirror) with you at all times. While you're talking to someone, take sips of water when the other person is speaking to ensure your mouth doesn't become dry. Use a breath spray or mints. I like a product called BreathRx Tongue Spray. Unlike those curiously strong mints that simply mask bad breath, BreathRx contains anti-bacterial ingredients to kill the bacteria causing the bad breath. I also recommend using a tongue scraper morning and night with BreathRx rinse, and after your coffee break to make your mouth conversation-ready. I'm sorry if I sound like an infomercial!

Okay, enough on this topic. You're ready. Now get out there and make the most of those conferences and trade shows.

3.4

The Networked Organization Action Plan

- Engage other attendees in a conversational, questioning style.
- Remember that booth workers often know people who could be of value to you. Get to know the booth workers.
- Use this as an opener: *So, what are you finding of greatest value at this conference/event/trade show?*
- Create a goal of meeting and providing value to at least five people at every conference or trade show.
- Head to the edges at loud parties and be cautious about your alcohol consumption.
- Make personal hygiene, e.g., having fresh breath with no dry mouth residue, a priority.

3.4

THE NETWORKING DINNER (OR LUNCH)

For those who ask, *Does everything have to be a networking event? Is there anything I can do to build relationships without going to a lot of major events?* Sure. Simply pulling together a group of people that you want to get to know better is a great way.

In his book *Never Eat Alone,* Keith Ferrazzi likes to call this "the art of the slow dinner." Ferrazzi says that breaking bread over a long, relaxed time does more to build relationships than most other activities. I agree. Nothing beats a great dinner party!

The dinner party doesn't need to be fancy, but it does need to have forethought. The perfect dinner party is 10 people. Eight is too few. Twelve is too many. You need to be strategic about where people sit. Have assigned seating with place cards and do not let couples sit next to each other. If you host the dinner at home, you could make it a pot luck where each person brings a dish or a beverage, all pre-planned ahead of time.

If you're really adventurous, you could do an *Open Kitchen* concept, where people bring ingredients and split up into small groups to make the salad, appetizers, main course, and dessert. Just make sure you have room and think about work space where the different dishes can be prepped, whether it's on the kitchen counter or on a couple of card tables that you set up. Cooking in groups is fun and can bring people together in unexpected ways.

I used to host a women's dinner almost every quarter. I connected with another woman and we agreed that we would both invite five interesting women to each dinner. We held our dinners at restaurants where we were able to reserve private rooms. Both of us got to meet people we didn't know previously. Even better, we didn't have to cook!

It doesn't always have to be dinner—and it doesn't always have to be a party.

3.5

Maybe it's 10 people. Maybe it's just three. Maybe it's asking two others to join you for lunch. Maybe the two people you're meeting are two people who don't know each other, but ought to meet. Already you're providing value by making the introduction.

I also regularly host lunches where I pull together a small group of executives who ought to know each other. I've been organizing such events for more than a decade. Sometimes I host five people. Sometimes 25. The only caveat is that everyone has to pay for their own meal.

Not every invitee requires a lot of forethought. A funny thing happens when you pull random people together. Somehow they find a connection. Somehow they end up believing that you already knew the reason they ought to meet.

How can you start this practice? Identify a couple people and invite them. Let them know in advance that they'll be paying for their own meal so there's no confusion. Let them know who else or what kind of people you're inviting.

You could organize around functional area, industry, business issue, or business model. If you want to get smarter in a certain industry or area, find people who are in that industry. Put together your list and start making calls.

Hey, I'm pulling together a group of people who care about [industry/ business issue/function] to grab lunch and we'd love to include you. One caveat: you have to pay for your own meal. Would you like to be included?

3.5

You could, and should, do this with others in your organization as well. Each month, identify and invite three to four different people to meet for lunch. Doing this both internally and externally will give you a real head start on executing your relationship portfolio.

When you're all around the table, then what? Remember to plan a handful of conversation starter questions in advance that will make people comfortable, help them engage, and end up driving thought-provoking and valuable conversation and relationships. I strongly suggest you stay away from politics or other topics that invite emotionally charged and conflicting opinions. Nobody enjoys having to defend their opinions in front of a new group of people, and bringing up a politically sensitive topic could do just that. Some conversation starter questions include:

- *Let's go around the table. Please introduce yourself and tell us what you're working on these days, and share with us something most people don't know about you.*
- *So, where are you all seeing the opportunities in [topic area]?*
- *What do you find most interesting about doing business here?*
- *Did anyone see the big game last night?*
- *Did you read about the [article in the paper]? What do you think?*
- *Who watched the finals of [tv show/game/reality competition]? Did you think that person was going to win?*
- *Who watched the semi-finals of [tv show / game / reality competition]? Who do you think is going to win?*
- *I'm looking for a good [ethnicity] restaurant, any ideas?*
- *What's your favorite [upcoming holiday] tradition?*
- *What's your favorite game on* The Price is Right? (I had to throw this one in!)

It doesn't have to be complicated. It doesn't have to be fancy. It just has to be implemented.

The Networked Organization Action Plan

- Schedule a dinner party. Ten is the ideal number to have at dinner. Have more to invite? Do two dinner parties.

- Choose your invitees with forethought on how they will contribute to building relationships among the attendees.

- Assign seating to ensure there is good opportunity for mingling. Spouses/partners should be seated apart from each other.

- For lunches, a smaller number, as few as two plus you, works.

- Let people know they're paying for their own lunch.

- End your invite with *Would you like to be included?* Everyone likes to be included.

3.5

NETWORKING
REFERRALS

If you ask most people how they find their business, they usually say much of it comes by word-of-mouth; that is, through referrals,

Does **EVERYONE** in your organization **KNOW** what a **GOOD CUSTOMER** looks like?

sometimes upwards of 80%. What's interesting to me is that most people spend more time on cold calling, advertising, and other marketing activities that rarely, if ever, result in a positive ROI than they do on building a good referral network.

If your organization receives much of its business from word-of-mouth or referrals, or you'd like to reduce your cost of customer acquisition, then it's time you start paying attention to how your team increases its referral base.

When I worked in marketing for IBM, I built a marketing economics model that showed each type of marketing and sales activity and its return on investment. Based on the model, you could determine how much money to put into each type of activity to drive the return you were looking for. The model demonstrated something that is really no surprise: using a salesperson to prospect (cold call, knock on doors) was cost-prohibitive and does nothing more than use your most expensive resource to generate awareness. But the model also showed how other forms of marketing can drive results, and therefore help determine how much money to spend in any one activity. Did my model make a difference? Not really, because at the time, IBM never really provided enough money at the regional level to make an impact. I did, however, eventually apply the concept at another company where I used the data to make decisions, and where we were able to do a great job of spending money on the right activities to drive a higher ROI.

After I left IBM, I ran corporate marketing departments. I employed the typical marketing tactics—lead generation campaigns, advertising, branding, collateral, public relations, trade shows, customer events, sales recognition programs, internet and intranet sites. And I did it all with a great team, a lot of hard work, and a minimal budget.

3.6

But given the option, would I do it the same way again? No. If I were to ever run marketing again, I would worry less about the program budget. I would worry less about the technology. I would worry less about the motivations.

Instead, I'd concern myself with one thing: Networking.

Are our employees well networked with others in the industry? With customers? With suppliers? With buyers? With competitors? With substitutes? It's Michael Porter's Five Forces Model all over again. How competitive are we really if we're not fully engaged in the ecosystem of our supply chain? If the organization is not well networked, well connected, well in-the-know, what can I do to facilitate such a change? Our organization would benefit more if we spent five hours producing five quality leads for our sales force than if we spent five hours producing a piece of marketing collateral that no one wants to read anyway.

And what about inside the organization? Are our employees well networked inside the organization? Do our teams function properly? Do people create processes that affect other people, and if so, do they do it with the other people in mind? Do people know how to get things done? Do people know whom to call when they need exceptions? Do people keep the flow of communication going so they can be on the front end of issues?

I think about how most companies spend their marketing dollars. It seems to me a lot of opportunity for improvement exists. If the majority of business comes from referrals or word-of-mouth, what if the majority of the marketing dollars were spent on building a referral/word-of-mouth network? Some people in marketing might not want to hear that. It's okay. It doesn't necessarily mean you need to change all of your activities. It simply means that you need to redefine how you implement those activities.

Conferences and trade shows, for example, are typically very costly, given hotel and conference fees, airfare, meals, booth space, and "critical" giveaways like the t-shirt, pen, and Slinky. Most companies spend 90% of their time on pre-conference/event logistics, but very little time on the activities that contribute to a better return on their investment. Train your teams on how to have a conversation with someone who comes to their booth or how to work the floor—that is, how to meet people from the other booths who could be good referral sources. Provide giveaways that, when taken, drive people

205

back to you to make a buying decision about your product or service. Create a coordinated follow-up plan for the people you meet at the conference that includes determining who is in what phase of the buying cycle. Don't assume everyone is in the going-to-make-a-decision-today phase. Most of this during and after-the-fact activity is left up to individuals. Most of this after-the-fact activity is done pretty poorly, if at all. Add it all up and you can see how an expensive conference or trade show becomes even more costly.

Where do your referrals come from?

You never know where your referrals will come from. I remember a few years back when I was building a new executive search business. I was talking to my friend Jamie about it, who suggested I meet with Susan. Susan and I met, but never did any search engagements together. A month later, I received a call from someone who Susan had referred. He told me that he was looking to hire some people and Susan had told him I could help. I met with him, and got the business.

It was funny, though. My first client in that area would come from a referral of a referral—with whom I'd never worked. Sometimes the path of the referral is not a straight line. And who cares, really, whether it's the people who are in a position to make a decision on your product or service themselves or know someone who can?

One day, I received a call at the office from a person selling headsets. He wanted to talk about our headset needs. I told him we were all set and that we really weren't a good prospect for him. *Oh no*, he said. *I'm sure you are.* I knew we weren't. *I'm not your target*, I told him, and then asked him the important questions. Was he focused on call centers? If anyone uses lots of headsets, it's call centers. Was he participating in call center networking groups, both in person and online? No. Was he using online tools like LinkedIn to do a search on people who run call center operations and who are typically the decision makers for headsets? Had he spoken to the individual who runs call center operations for his own company to see who s/he knew? No, he hadn't, he said, but he thought they were all great ideas and he would implement them. When I told him I was sorry we couldn't buy anything from him, he said, *Molly, this is the best call I've made all day.*

This type of call happens all day, every day. Who is training these people? Who is helping them make a sale? What kind of lists are they giving them? Why don't they teach these people how to build a network and then work that network? Why are they wasting my time, their time, and their company's time…and money?

Referring people is risky.

A certain level of risk is inherent when referring others. Most people don't know how to act once they're in front of a prospect. Once I made some introductions for a few salespeople from a technology firm. One of the salespeople called me before the meeting to ask me how long I thought his presentation should be. At which point I freaked out! Are you kidding me? This is your first meeting with this potential customer and you think you're going to do a presentation? How do you even know your solution is one that will work for this company? What kind of rookie salesperson are you? Perhaps your time might be better spent getting to know the customer and building the foundation of a relationship. People typically buy from people they like. Why don't we get them to like you first?

After about three of those conversations, I decided we had a bigger problem with the referral: People don't know how to behave once they have a referral in a way that will generate more referrals.

Referrals versus introductions: Which is better?

That's easy. An introduction is better. That is, if it actually happens.

While an introduction may seem like the better route, a referral puts the control in your hands. With a referral, you have the ability to control the timing and the message.

> My friend Alex tells me he is very excited because he's spoken with an ex-colleague who is going to introduce Alex to the president of a company. *That's great,* I tell him. Two weeks go by. That may not seem like a long time, but as each day passes and more and more work builds up, the introduction Alex is looking for may be receiving less and less attention from his friend. When I ask Alex what he's waiting for, he tells me that his friend will get back to him as soon as he's had a chance to make the introduction.

This was a great lead for Alex. Yet he put all the control and ownership of it into someone else's hands and, more importantly, onto someone else's timeline. Naturally, he doesn't want to pester his friend too much for fear that he'll lose the introduction—which can definitely happen.

What should Alex have done? Instead of looking for an introduction, Alex might have better positioned himself with a referral. What's the difference? An *introduction* is when someone does just that—introduces you to someone…and controls the conversation by controlling your ability to connect with a contact. A *referral* is when you get someone's name from a friend or acquaintance, and you control the conversation by owning the follow-up. What if your friend doesn't give you the contact's phone number? Not a problem. Just ask where the person works, and pick up the phone and call that person's office.

I'm sure Alex's friend would have been fine letting Alex control the follow-up. If for some reason your friend really wants to make the introduction, then set some expectations. Say that you really appreciate it, and you'll plan to follow up directly with the referral by a certain date [name a date that is within five business days]. Then, if they haven't had time to control the introduction, you're not stuck in a position of waiting and waiting and waiting.

How to make an introduction

If you are going to take the time to introduce someone, here's how you might want to do it.

Preferably, call the person and say, *Chris, do you know Maria Gvardeitseva? I know her through _____. And I've been thinking about you and believe she's someone you really ought to know. I'm going to have her give you a call and set up some time. Thanks.*

3.6

Be sure to make the introduction about the person and not about the subject. If you make it about the subject, then your contact might find objections as to why he's not available or offer up suggestions as to why someone else in the organization would be a better person to meet. Maybe that person would be better. Maybe not.

If you decide to do an email intro, maybe it looks something like this:

> To: chris@email.com; maria@email.com
> **Subject:** Intro Maria/Chris
>
> Chris/Maria,
>
> You two ought to meet.
>
> Maria, Chris runs a very innovative company called Coolco. They're just beginning the discussion around international expansion.
>
> Chris, Maria is doing some really interesting work getting companies global visibility.
>
> Given what you're both trying to accomplish, I know you would enjoy a conversation.
>
> Here is your respective contact info:
>
> Chris Boone
> +1 (415) 555-5555
> chris@email.com
>
> Maria Gvardeitseva
> +375 (17) 55-5515
> maria@email.com
>
> Thanks for taking the time.
>
> Regards,
> Molly

3.6

Here's another example:

> To: jonathan@email.com; michelle@email.com
> Subject: Intro John/Michelle
>
> You two ought to meet.
>
> Michelle—I wanted to introduce you to John Whalley, a chief technology officer with major experience in health care, manufacturing, and insurance, among other industries. John ran his own healthcare focused turnaround consulting firm for a number of years. When he mentioned he had background in cloud strategy and implementation, I thought you ought to meet, as there could be mutual value for you two to have a chat. John can be reached at 555-555-1515.
>
> John—Michelle Warford is CEO of Valley Integration and is one of those impressive people you tend to remember. Based on our discussion of your experience with a variety of industries and cloud strategy, I think you two will have a lot to talk about. Michelle can be reached at 555-555-5155.
>
> I hope you two can carve out time for a chat soon.
>
> Regards,
>
> Tom

3.6

Networking Pitfall:
The referral inquisition

Nothing's worse than giving a referral, and then getting the equivalent of the Spanish Inquisition as to the strategy of how one should approach this person.

> Steve has a friend who wants to speak with someone at a company where I used to work. Once I understand which group he wants to talk to, I give him the contact information for Jeff. About two months later, I get a call from Steve who wants to know "the strategy" of how to approach Jeff.

Strategy? What strategy? You know I used to work with him. Here's a strategy: Pick up the phone, dial his number and say, *Is Jeff there? Molly Wendell suggested I reach out.*

The next time someone gives you a referral, don't be high maintenance. Ask how they know each other, get their contact information and cut the cord. Don't forget to follow up with a quick note saying, *Thank you for the referral. We met. It was great!*

Getting more referrals

> One day, I partially tear my right hamstring. How does this happen? Nothing dramatic, really. I am helping my niece, Maura, learn to ride a two-wheeler. Maura isn't pedaling very fast, so keeping up with her is easy. Then, all of a sudden, her confidence building, she takes off. I am running as fast as I can at the same time I am trying to maintain a hold on the seat to keep her upright. A few seconds later, I hear the tear...and feel the pain.

I had heard of Active Release Therapy (ART), a method to speed up healing. I find Dr. Nathan Campbell, a sports therapist/ART practitioner. In less than two months, my hamstring is healed.

As Dr. Campbell works on my hamstring we start talking about his business. I ask him how he got his clients. Mostly through referral, he says, but he is also in a networking group that meets weekly. *How long have you been in the group?* I ask. *How often do you meet? How many clients have you gotten from the group?* He's been in it more than a year. He meets weekly for one and a half hours, not including drive time, and he's gotten a whopping five clients.

That's about the time I freak out!

WHHHHHAAAAAATTTTTT??????? I want to shout. What are you thinking? Do you realize you've just spent more than 70 hours of your life producing five clients? Do you have any idea how much that's cost you? Give me five hours and *I'll* find you five clients. Because, really, everyone I know has some type of injury that could probably be healed with ART. Just hang out with a bunch of weekend warriors and you've got a client base for life.

That's when Dr. Campbell and I start talking about the value of networking, and about how to approach it from a more efficient standpoint. Too many people do the activities that others do, thinking they'll get the same results. Maybe they do get the same results. But maybe they should question the effectiveness of the results to begin with.

Now, I'm not knocking these weekly referral groups. Well, maybe I am. But if I'm in a group and I'm not getting at least one lead a week, then I'm hanging out with the wrong referral group. In turn, if I'm in a group and not providing at least one lead a week to the majority of people in that group, I'm not an effective referral source for them. If that's the case, my seat at the table should go to someone else.

Everyone in the group is looking for leads and should have the attitude that they want to give a lot and get a lot. Most people I know who join groups like this, however, have the same experience as Dr. Campbell. For example, I used to do work with a national site selection company for meeting planners. At that time, the big trend for the salespeople was to join one of these referral groups. After one person got one lead from a group like this, the concept spread like wildfire throughout the company. But over and over, I saw the same results. Lots of hours spent driving to and attending these meetings, and not a lot of business to show for it.

Be ready to
LEVERAGE
the right
OPPORTUNITIES
when they present
themselves.

3.6

Honestly, when you do the math and look at the return on investment, you're probably better off standing outside the grocery store wearing a sandwich board and catching the draft from the Girl Scout's cookie sale.

So, how do you do it? How do you get leads, if not from a lead referral group?

Leads are like air. They're everywhere. Unlike air, they're not a free commodity. You have to be in the right place. You have to be equipped with the right conversation. You have to be ready to leverage the right opportunities when they present themselves.

My family is taking a break from the heat while vacationing in Dubai. While at the Mall of Dubai, I ask a passerby if he'll take our picture. Turns out, Don Smith is in Dubai looking at retail spaces for Michael's Cookies, a San Diego-based cookie company. As we get to talking, my husband asks him about their plans for India. Don says they'd love to get a foothold in India. My husband connects Don with Siddhartha Hegde, founder of Coffee Day, the largest coffee conglomerate in India with retail stores throughout. Now Don is in discussions to distribute his cookies through the hottest coffee shop in India. Not a bad return for the investment in time of taking a tourist's picture.

How are you equipping others in your organization to be good referral sources?

I talked earlier about how organizations are trying to collaborate with other divisions—to share contacts and opportunities. There's so much more to be done in this area.

Does everyone in your organization know what a good customer looks like? How are you ensuring that they do? How are you ensuring that everyone in the organization understands the value of being intentional around identifying potential new customers? What are you putting in place to reward those who get on board? Those who are intentional around networking? Those who identify opportunity for the organization even if it isn't "their job" to do so?

Many organizations today have great referral programs to help find new talent. But how many have an orchestrated program to assist those who have on-going interaction with customers to find new business? Maybe it's your field service organization. Maybe it's your customer service team. They can be a great source of referrals.

What if everyone in the company had a better grasp of the target customer profile and why they buy from you?

Tom Smith (yes, that's his real name) really gets this networked organization concept. At IBM, he was charged with turning around a $140M services organization. He knew he needed to better leverage the entire team and identify as many new opportunities for the sales team as possible.

When Tom observed that customers often put the most trust in the field service personnel—the people who fix equipment—he created a training program to teach the field service technicians not how to sell, but simply how to identify potential opportunities. He taught them the following three things: (1) to understand the valuable role they played in helping turn around the organization; (2) to understand the basics of a relationship building conversation; and (3) most important, to ask their customers three questions, which would in turn identify opportunities:

1. *How often do you update your software?*
2. *How often do you apply the software fixes that are delivered to you each month?*
3. *Who updates the software?*

What the service technicians found is that because customers didn't update their software often enough, they were experiencing software problems for which they already had fixes onsite. The technicians also found that the people responsible for applying the updates and fixes were overwhelmed with other projects, making updates a lower priority. That is, until the software failed.

When the software failed, the service technicians informed their managers, who got the sales team involved. In a few short months, the business took off, with more than 50 new opportunities identified by only half of the technicians.

Referrals are not just for business-to-business organizations.

Let's say you work for a consumer goods company that traditionally acquires customers differently from a company that sells to businesses. How much thought have you given to the idea of referral-based networking? It seems like a monumental task, which is possibly why consumer-focused companies typically spend more of their marketing budget on advertising and branding. But is it possible that its very own workforce could make a difference? Let's think about that.

With the advent of social media, many consumer brands have also put a fair amount of resource and energy into building communities. But they typically focus that energy into the corporate Facebook, LinkedIn, and Twitter sites.

What if, say, Coca-Cola, with its 130,000 employees, started leveraging its own employees' social spheres of influence in an intentional way. Take Facebook alone, where the average number of friends by Facebook users from 25-65 years old is approximately 250. Coca-Cola's reach, through employees alone, would be approximately 32 Million. That reach is about 30% of the Super Bowl audience at a significantly reduced price. And what if the social sphere could influence its "friends" to consume one additional Coca-

3.6

3.6

Now this is something to smile about.

Leveraging your employees' social spheres of influence could reach a significant audience and have a major impact on overall growth.

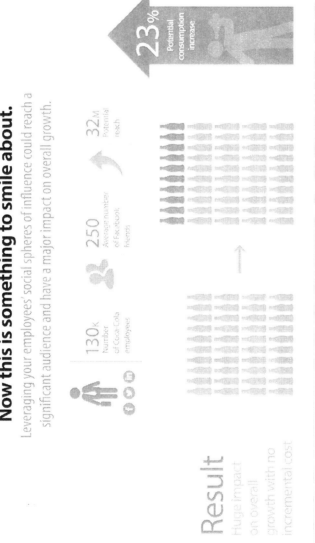

130k
Number of Coca-Cola employees

250
Average Number of Facebook friends

32M
Potential reach

23%
Potential consumption increase

Result

Huge impact on overall growth with no incremental cost

What about your organization?

250
Friends

Number of employees

Potential reach

Cola beverage per month? That would generate a 23% increase in overall consumption. That could have a huge impact on the overall growth of the organization. And that number doesn't even include pass-along rate—the percentage of people who pass along the message to their network.

Maybe it's time to take inventory of your employee's social circles and see how your organization might benefit. Among Facebook, LinkedIn, and Twitter, you may find that you have a massive referral opportunity right in front of you.

But don't make them do it on their own. Have a coordinated effort. Refer back to our conversation on Corporate Social Branding and put some consistency around it. Ask marketing to supply content your teams can post on Facebook, LinkedIn, and Twitter at their discretion. Catalog these posts on your corporate intranet. Make it easy for your teams to copy/paste the information to their own social profiles. Include a picture or video. Make it fun. Make it interesting. Make it relevant. Make it easy.

You have to start somewhere.

3.6

I receive a lot of phone calls from people trying to tap into our network and sell their services. Over and over, I let them know that we're not the right fit for their sales pitch. But here's the funny thing. For every person who calls, if I really thought about it, most likely I could come up with five people—whether friends, colleagues or acquaintances—who could probably benefit from their services. If the people who called me built a relationship with me, I just might be inclined to send business their way. Instead, most of them hang up and I never hear from them again.

It reminds me of a rookie football player. Would you show up in the beginning of football season and expect to play in the Super Bowl? Of course not. You know you'd have to earn it week in and week out. That each successful week would bring you that much closer to making the playoffs—and that your continued success would land you a spot as the star of one of the most-watched sporting events on television.

My advice? Quit trying to go for the big win before you've ever played a game.

Start with building a relationship one-on-one. How do you start building a relationship? Go to a networking event that includes logical referral types. If you're an accountant, hang out with some lawyers, and vice versa. Are you in human resources? Start attending finance-oriented events. Are you in the consumer space? Create content for your employees to deliver to their social circles.

Get involved in a charity. Get involved in an association. Start a meet-up oriented around a topic of interest. Do something to get with like-minded people with whom you can build the foundations of a relationship. Once those relationships are solid, you'll be on much firmer ground to get help in your business. Your newfound friends really want to help you succeed.

I know I've said it before, but don't think this advice is strictly for sales teams. It's for everyone in the organization. Imagine if all team members were focused on building a good referral network. Imagine if all team members were intentional in their activities to identify new prospects and pass them onto the sales organization. Now you can begin to imagine what it's like to work for a Networked Organization.

You've heard it said that people buy from people they like. Well, people refer people they like, too. Get engaged. Get connected. Build relationships. Then, hold on for the ride. Just make sure my niece and her two-wheeler aren't at the helm!

3.6

The Networked Organization Action Plan

- Get referrals, not introductions.
- Take inventory of your organizations' "true" social sphere of influence and build programs to leverage it.
- Create a group of like-minded people.
- Enable your field service organization with relationship training and key opportunity-identification questions.
- Show people you're referral worthy.

3.6

THE RELATIONSHIP
PROCESS

4.1

Extending Networked
Relationships:
Getting a Meeting

As you practice these networking techniques you'll find that you meet a lot of people and end up with a lot of acquaintances. What extends a relationship and takes it to another level is taking it through the relationship process and building it through more in-depth interaction. Preferably, this interaction is face-to-face. The next best alternative is a phone call. These days, people make the mistake of trying to build a relationship over email or text, which, again, may seem efficient, but actually is not all that effective. Now is about the time someone usually chimes in and says, *But I connected with someone online and have a great relationship.* Yes, I'm sure you do. But can you imagine how much greater it might be if you shook hands in person, sat down, and had a meaningful conversation, one where you could read the non-verbal cues?

You might ask yourself, *Why would this person want to meet with me?* The better question is, *Why wouldn't they want to meet with you?* Aren't you a good person? Aren't you worthy of being known? Don't

4.1

you have value to offer? Well then, let them get to know you. I say this, of course, with the thought that their getting to know you is accomplished by your getting to know them.

Moving the relationship forward

Sometimes you want to get a meeting with someone you met at a networking event. Other times, it's someone on your target list (the one you built from Section 2.1, The Intentional Network: Building Your Relationship Portfolio). And still other times, it could be someone at your organization.

When speaking with others about people you want to meet, remember what my sixth-grade English teacher always said. *To be specific is terrific. To be vague is the plague.* Don't say, *Do you know anyone I should meet?* Figure out what industry they're from; what companies they worked for. Ask to be referred to people who are likely in their network.

How to get a meeting with anyone

What's the easiest way to get a meeting? Get a referral. What do you do if you don't have one? Get one.

4.1

What if you still don't have one? Try harder.

Now what?

Well, here's what you *don't* do. You don't try to meet with them via email.

Most people I know consider themselves in-person per-sons—meaning they make a better impression in person than they do over the phone or email. Yet, so many people these days try to start and build relationships using a method that does not best represent them.

So often, when I ask people if they've connected with one of their networking targets, they say, *I sent an email. I haven't heard back.* Maybe the person you emailed never got the email. Maybe it's buried in her inbox. Do you realize how many emails people get? Do you realize how easy it is to hide behind email? Of course you do. You may be guilty of it yourself.

Instead of sending an email, do something really crazy. Pick up the phone. Call that person. But be smart about it. Be sure to make the meeting about the person and not the company. And definitely use my renowned call/call/email approach. Here's what that looks like.

Make the first call when you don't believe they'll be there. Maybe call their office line between 6 and 8 p.m. Leave a message like this:

> "Hi Bill, this is Molly Wendell. Carol McDaid suggested I give you a call to set up a time to meet. I'm relatively new to the aerospace industry and Carol said if there's anyone who could give me insight into the industry, it's you. I'm really looking forward to meeting you. I can be reached at 312-123-4567. Again, my number is 312-123-4567. Thank you."

WARNING! Bill may actually pick up the phone, so be prepared to ask for a meeting.

After this first message, will Bill call you back? Probably not. So, call again. This time, call at a time when you believe Bill will be in the office, maybe three days later, preferably on a Thursday or Friday afternoon. These are the days of the week when people are most open to a conversation. They also typically have their schedule for the next week pretty well set, so they'll know their availability. This call sounds something like this:

> "Hi Bill. Molly Wendell again, referred by Carol McDaid. I'm really looking forward to meeting with you. Tell you what. I'm going to send you an email with some possible dates and times. If it's easier to get back to me that way, then great. Otherwise, I can be reached at 312-123-4567. Again, 312-123-4567."

Notice how I don't go into the why the way I did on the first message, but focus more on the when. It moves the conversation to a scheduling discussion. This way, you've given Bill a heads up to watch out for your email. To get someone's email, ask your referral source, call the company and confirm it, or check online to see how emails are structured at that company. Take a look at their press releases and see how they format the public relation's contact. Try googling "lastname@company.com" with the lastname@company website in quotes. That might get you the format. Sometimes to figure out the format, I google smith@companyname.com because most companies have at least one person with the last name of Smith. Also, bcc other formats you think might be correct like firstinitiallast@company.com.

Common Email Formats

4.1

Full name	johndoe@company.com
First initial Last name	jdoe@company.com
First name dot Last name	john.doe@company.com
First name underscore Last name	john_doe@company.com
First name (early-stage companies)	john@company.com

This is what your email looks like (notice the signature line contains both a phone number and email address):

SUBJECT: Ref'd by Carol McDaid

Bill,

I'm really looking forward to getting a few minutes of your time. I'm new to the aerospace industry and Carol said if there's anyone who could give me insight into the industry, it's you.

Do any of these times work for you: Tues., 11/25 or Wed., 11/26, any time after 10 a.m. ET?

If not, please let me know what would.

Thank you,
Molly Wendell
312-123-4567
info@mollywendell.com

At this point, chances are good Bill will respond. If he doesn't respond in a timely manner, say two to three weeks, try again. If after that, you still have no response, go back to your referral and ask for help. Remember, Carol didn't give me Bill's info because Carol didn't want a meeting to happen. The key is to make the meeting about the person, not the company. That way they can't send you to someone else in the company.

> Make the meeting about
> **THE PERSON,**
> not the company.

4.1

WARNING! If your contact offers to have the conversation over the phone, simply say, *Oh, I'd much rather meet in person. When's a good time?* Do your best not to meet people over the phone unless you absolutely must due to geographic constraints. If there's ever a way to meet in person in the future, do so. Even if it means the meeting is six months out. You'll almost always make more progress in person than over the phone.

When you leave a message, be sure to include your phone number. How often do you receive messages from people who don't leave their contact information? Sometimes people don't even leave a message because they're waiting to get you live. Perhaps you just missed the call and could've returned it right away, but now can't because they didn't leave a number, or even a message. Sometimes, you receive more focused time and attention when they can talk to you on their schedule versus when you try to reach them on yours.

Getting a meeting is that easy. I've employed this strategy for every meeting I've ever wanted. And I've met with hundreds, bordering on thousands, of people. Believe me, it works. And it's a lot more effective and a lot less frustrating than waiting for an email response that may or may not show up.

Here's a funny story that reminds us that sometimes people actually pick up the phone when we're least expecting it. My husband is trying to connect with Bill and even has a referral. We are up late one night, and he's rehearsing the message he is going to leave. He has a bit of trouble getting to Bill's voicemail because he doesn't have his direct phone number. After a few tries, we figure out how to get to a company directory and type in Bill's name. I leave him to his own devices. He comes upstairs a couple minutes later, and I ask how it went. *Horrible,* he says, *He answered his phone! It's 2:00 am and he answers his phone!* I said, *Oh my gosh, I hope you just hung up. No,* he said, *I wasn't thinking and went right into my spiel, Hi Bill, this is Tom, Judy suggested I reach out....* All we could do was laugh. So, again, a word of warning, be careful when you call, because Bill may just pick up the phone!

Cold calling

Don't! Just don't! Be very un-Nike-like. Don't do it! You know what people are thinking when the phone rings? *Who are you and why are you wasting my time?* It may carry a different tone when they say hello. It may not. Think quickly, because that's what it's going to take to give them a good reason to not hang up.

Some people are really good at cold calling. They're probably the same people who've made millions of dollars teaching other people how to do it. The percentage of people who excel at cold calling is low. Very low.

Why put yourself in that position? Why not have some credibility from the start? Instead of cold calling, get a referral to that person. A referral will usually buy you the extra seconds you need to get what you want out of the call.

> Learn from my friend David. David tells me about a great client he is hoping to get. It has his name written all over it, and he's very excited about it. With a little research, David figures out that he and Jeff, the person making the decision, went to the same graduate school. Instead of getting a referral, David thinks that knowing the same fight song of their alma mater will be enough. Little does he know that it won't even be close.
>
> David makes the call, immediately references the fact that Jeff and he went to the same school, and hopes for the best. What happens is the worst. Jeff answers the phone with a tone that says he is bothered by the interruption. If he was so busy, why did he answer? David makes some one-sided small talk about the school, and then brings up the opportunity. Jeff immediately, for whatever reason, decides David's firm isn't a fit, and ends the call. That quickly. Game over.

4.1

What could David have done differently? First and foremost, David could've found someone who knew Jeff, either through a work or school connection. Then, the call could have sounded something like this: *Jeff, my name is David. Kammie Kobyleski told me to call you. I work in big data analytics and we got to talking about what you're doing. Kammie really thinks the world of you and thinks we ought to meet. When might be a good time?*

Right now, Jeff is feeling pretty good about himself because Kammie said something nice about him. His attitude is positive. He's probably more open to a discussion. And because the call was focused on a meeting that was Kammie's idea, Jeff is more likely to make some time. If Jeff asks why they should meet, David can refer back to Kammie. *Oh, you know Kammie. If she says we ought to meet, we'd better do so.* And during a face-to-face meeting, David can start building his own relationship.

What do you do when someone won't meet with you?

It's a rare occasion that someone won't meet with you when you have a referral. Still, if this happens, call the person who referred you and tell them the situation. *I was really looking forward to meeting John, but he says he doesn't have time.* At that point, the referrer can call John and request that he try to find some time to meet with you. If your referrer doesn't think of that, feel free to suggest it. They didn't give you the referral for it to not come through. They want to help.

I've had only one person turn me down for a meeting, at least initially. It was even a referral. I called Mike, used my reference, Becky, and suggested a meeting. Mike told me he didn't have time. I called Becky and told her. *I was really looking forward to meeting Mike, but he says he doesn't have time.* She told me to call Mike back and tell him that she said he had to meet with me. Remember, people don't give you referrals for them not to come through. They want to help. So I did what Becky said. Amazing how quickly Mike's schedule freed up. He and I met the following week. There was definitely extra pressure to ensure I made it worth his time.

If you're finding that people won't meet with you despite a referral, then you're either getting referred by the wrong people who don't carry the necessary social capital, or your approach needs a revision.

When you're looking to build relationships, quit thinking that placing a call or sending an email is enough to get them engaged. Instead, get a referral. Turn that cold call into a warm call. Now it's time to be very Nike-like. Just do it!

Scheduling meetings

When it comes to scheduling, sometimes you don't have a choice. You're at the mercy of someone else's calendar. Or are you? If you have the choice, keep this in mind. People are more likely to change meetings on Mondays or Tuesdays than any other day of the week. If you want to minimize changes, schedule meetings for later in the week. Friday afternoon is typically the best time to talk to people and catch them when they're most open-minded, but typically the worst time to head out into traffic. Don't schedule your meetings to start or end during peak commute time if you feel inconvenienced by that. Obviously the time has to work for the person you're meeting with, but it also has to work for you. Make the experience enjoyable, not a chore.

Once you get the meeting scheduled, send a calendar invite to ensure it's on your respective calendars.

4.1

What if someone cancels? Usually, I'm okay with people cancelling, unless it's short notice and I'm coming in from another city; then I'm not okay. If I have a day or two's cancellation notice for a local conversation, that's pretty easy to reschedule. Plus, it puts you at an advantage. When people cancel, they feel bad. They want to make it up to you. I don't mind when people feel as if they owe me a favor or two.

A quick confirmation call, email, or text two to three days prior to your meeting is always a good idea. It could be as simple as this: *Looking forward to seeing you Friday, 6/22, 2:00 PM at your office.*

I rarely schedule breakfast meetings, because I don't really like breakfast…or traffic. I once broke my rule and scheduled a breakfast meeting. It was a trek for me to get there, about 30 miles in morning traffic. I waited at the restaurant all alone for an hour before calling it quits. Turns out the person had been let go the Friday before and didn't have a copy of his calendar. How do you not have a copy of your calendar?

If you think you might be inconvenienced due to a cancellation, try to plan the meeting in a way that puts the least amount of potential inconvenience on you. Schedule multiple meetings on the same day/same location/back-to-back.

4.1

It's time for your meeting. Now what?

What's your goal? How about something simple like getting them to like you? Much can happen when people like you. Not much will if they don't.

The onus is on you to make it worth their time. You may have some objectives you'd like to get out of meeting, and one of them better be: *Figure out how to help this person—through a lead, contact, or idea.*

Show up on time, or a little early, dressed appropriately. Don't show up like you just came from the gym. Todd did that to me. Want to know how much I helped Todd? I didn't. What was his message to me? I'm not important enough for him to put some business clothes on, let alone take a shower. Maybe my referral won't be important enough either. I can't take the chance.

Hot tip: If you go to Starbucks, the line is significantly shorter at 20 after and 10 til the hour. Instead of spending all of your networking time in line, go there at 10 til the hour, get a table, get your drink, and be ready when your appointment shows up. If they have to stand in line, join them or wait at the table and go through your notes one last time. Better yet, call or text them and say *I got here early. What can I get you to drink?* If you've never met the person face-to-face, you might also add, *I have a blue shirt on and am at a table close to the door.*

Have pen and paper available. Thank them for meeting you and give them a little background. Very little. Then, start with the smart questions you're going to read about in the next section.

4.1

The Networked Organization Action Plan

- Avoid cold calling by getting referrals.
- Use Molly's renowned Call/Call/Email Approach.
- Schedule the meeting for a time that's mutually convenient.
- Remember, the onus is on you to make the meeting worth their time.

4.1

4.2

Smart Networking
Questions

Be interesting by being interested.

SMART
questions lead to
INSIGHT
into how you can
HELP OTHERS.

If you're looking for the silver bullet in this book, congratulations, you found it. Say hello to *Molly's Smart Networking Questions*!

It's not your answers that define you, but instead your questions. The problem is that people are generally more concerned with what they're going to say versus what they're going to ask. But building deeper relationships is really about the ask. It's about asking the right questions to get to know people better. It's about asking smart questions. And smart questions take time. Smart questions take critical thinking skills. Delivering thought-provoking questions at just the right moment takes practice.

You may be the best door opener, the person with the greatest handshake, but if you get in there and talk too much or ask the mundane, your credibility and opportunity go right out the window.

> Show what you know by the QUESTIONS you ask, not the ANSWERS you give.

The smartest tool I ever implemented

The smartest thing I ever did when I ran corporate marketing for a technology consulting firm was to produce company-logoed spiral bound notebooks for our entire field sales organization.

The dumbest thing I ever did was to not teach the sales organization how to use them. Maybe it seems obvious, but I didn't even think about it at the time. After all, who doesn't know how to use a notebook? What I should have done was train the people on how to use the single greatest sales tool and marketing tactic available: a blank sheet of paper!

That blank sheet of paper is for writing down your questions, and their answers.

4.2

Have you ever been to a restaurant where the server stands there ready to take your order, but doesn't have a pen or paper? *Don't worry*, he says. *I'll remember it.* Yeah, right. You'll remember it like I'll remember your name, which you told me about two seconds ago, but I've already forgotten.

My order sounds something like this: *Yes, I'll have a burger, medium rare. Does it come with pepper jack cheese? Okay. And no onions. And instead of the fries, can I have a salad? Okay. No onions, okay? And I'll take ranch dressing on the side. Did you get the no-onions part? Are you sure you're going to remember this? Do you want to write it down? No? Okay. Well, please don't let them overcook my burger. Thanks.*

Here's what shows up. A burger cooked medium-well piled high with onions and a side of fries. I get a side salad, but it too has onions. The waiter's forgotten what kind of dressing I wanted, so he has to go back for it. It doesn't really matter, though, because I end up having to send the whole thing back. Every time. Every. Time.

I've gotten to the point where, if the server doesn't want to write it down, I offer to do it for him. Servers seem to take pride in not writing my order down. Perhaps they might take more pride in getting my order correct the first time.

While you're trying to show that you have the memory of an elephant, what you're really showing is you have the behavior of a donkey. There's no pride is showing off your memory skills. The pride resides in being positioned for success.

Here's an idea. Write all your questions on one page and leave room for answers on another page. That way, your list of questions remains easy to read and uncluttered. If you don't want to write the whole question, use a key word to prompt you. Do whatever works for you, as long as your method includes using a pen and paper.

4.2

Next, when you ask someone a question, be prepared to listen to the answer. You need to be perceived as someone who listens. You need to be prepared to write it down.

When I'm on an airplane, I don't sit there pen in hand ready to take notes, but if something comes up that I want to capture, I certainly take a notebook out of my bag and write it down. I'll say something like, *Oh, I want to remember that. I'm going to write that down.* When I'm meeting with someone, I have a notebook. When I'm at a networking event, I am prepared with my NetNotes to take notes.

When I worked at IBM, Pam Meijers, my teammate, and I ran focus groups with our sales teams to better understand what they were looking for from the marketing team. I led the groups and Pam took the notes. One particular sales leader had real issues with me and I couldn't figure out why. One day we were having a heart to heart. *Randy, I just don't understand why you have such a problem with me. What have I done?* He looked at me. *Molly,* he said, *you don't listen. You just don't listen. Pam, she listens. She's a great listener.* And that's when it hit me. He thinks I don't listen because I don't write anything down. He thinks Pam is a great listener because she writes everything down. The funny thing is that Pam would tell you she has a less than stellar memory and liked to write everything down so she didn't forget it. I am just the opposite. I pretty much remembered everything. I didn't need to write it down.

Or did I?

From that day forward, I started taking notes. I took notes everywhere I went, every meeting, every interaction. I never again wanted to be wrongfully accused of not listening.

4.2

If you're in a role where it's important to be a good listener—and by that I mean if you work anywhere—then start taking notes when other people are speaking. When you take notes people perceive that you are a good listener.

If you're at a conference or in a training class, the presenter sees who is taking notes and who is not. If you're in a team meeting, the manager sees who is taking notes and who is there for the doughnuts. If you're in a one-on-one meeting, the other person has a better impression of you because you are displaying a vested interest in what that person has to say.

I can't emphasize this idea enough. If you think you have a good memory, good for you. Try out for the game show *Jeopardy!* If you *know* you have a good memory, remember that life is not always about what you remember from the conversation, but how you are perceived during the conversation.

Don't be wrongfully accused. Show you're a good listener by taking good notes.

Questions that build relationships

You have to be good at asking questions in order to be good at building relationships. It helps to have a natural curiosity about people. Even if you don't, it's a skill you can learn. Asking questions doesn't mean you don't prepare. It simply means that you prepare in a different way. Be thoughtful about the questions you want to ask.

Most people are pretty bad at asking questions. They get too detailed. They dig deep in the trenches or ask close-ended questions that stop conversations in their tracks. When you think about your questions, always keep the other person in mind. What do they care about? What's important to them? Show you've done your homework. Show what you know by the questions you ask.

4.2

I'm sitting next to a man from Cerner on the plane. Cerner is a big technology company focused primarily on healthcare information systems. They run many of the systems that hospitals use. As soon as he tells me he's from Cerner, I say, *Wow, your company is doing some really interesting things. Can you give me a little more insight into the data analytics you're using to help hospitals provide better care for patients?* That's all Steve needs. He takes off and goes on for about 40 minutes. I continue to pepper him with additional questions here and there. Finally he says, *You're pretty familiar with the industry. Which healthcare company do you work for?* I tell him I don't work in healthcare, but I have a lot of friends who do. That's true, but more so, the week before, I'd read an article about Cerner in *Fortune* magazine. It was a really good article, which obviously gave me just enough information to ask the right questions.

Questions that break the ice

Whether I'm on an airplane or at a networking function, I use the same general questions, similar to the ones I talked about earlier. I use those same questions every time because they get a conversation started. You can develop your own set of questions or use mine. The key is to be consistent. Make it easy for you to remember. Practice doesn't necessarily make perfect, but it does make permanent. The first time you deliver these questions it might seem rehearsed, but the hundredth time you deliver the same ones, they'll come out naturally. You want to seem at ease in a relationship setting. When you're at ease, people perceive you to be more confident. If asking the same seven questions of everyone makes you more at ease, you'll feel more comfortable and natural in a networking setting.

Regardless of the fact that you ask the same thing, every conversation is going to be different because every person you meet has different answers.

Take a look at the Questions That Start Relationships chart to get some ideas on how to formulate your questions.

Questions That Start Relationships

Purpose	Goal	Types of Questions
Networking Events	Break the ice. Find out who they know. Get them to like you so they'll open up their network to you.	• General in nature • Non-threatening • Conversation openers
One-on-one	Learn about the person/company/industry. Find out who they know. Get them to like you so they'll open up their network to you.	• Specific/relevant • Inquisitive • Borderline bold
The Interview	Learn about the company strategy. Determine if it aligns with your objectives. Get them to like you and to think you're the right person for the job.	• Thought-provoking • Strategic • Bold
The Airplane	Break the ice. Learn about the person/company/industry. Find out who they know. Get them to like you so they'll open up their network to you.	• General in nature • Non-threatening • Conversation openers
Conferences	Break the ice. Learn about the person/company/industry. Get them to like you so they'll open up and share their insights.	• General in nature • Non-threatening • Conversation openers

4.2

Your goal in any networking interaction is threefold:

- Get them to like you.
- Figure out how you can help them.
- Determine if they are people with whom you'd like to build a relationship.

Molly's Top 7 "Back Pocket" Questions

When a networking opportunity presents itself, these are the questions I like to keep handy in my back pocket. You should consider keeping them in your back pocket, too.

1. *What do you do?*
2. *Who do you work for?*
3. *How long have you been there?*
4. *And where were you before that?*
5. *And how long were you there?*
6. *And where were you before that?*
7. *And how long were you there?*

Questions 6 and 7 are repeats of 4 and 5. And 4 and 5 are reworded versions of questions 3 and 4. If you can memorize the first three, you'll be set.

4.2

Again, if I'm on the airplane, I use these questions, but start with a different one: *Are you going home or going away?* Which then leads to Question 1: *What do you do?*

With these questions, you're simply trying to figure out what a person's network looks like. Try to gather about 10 to 12 years' work experience. If someone says she worked at company A for five years, and company B for 20, don't bother asking where she was before that. If you've worked at three different companies in three different industries in the last 10 years, you probably have a more well-rounded network. I find that people who work for the same company 20 years or more tend to have pretty narrow networks. Sure, there are exceptions to this rule, but in general, it's a safe assumption.

Obviously, when you're extending the relationship and meeting someone one-on-one, you don't want to ask the same questions you asked when you first met them.

My husband's favorite question is: *What compelled you to join [company]?* Then he follows it up with: *What about the organization or role did you not expect going in?* Or at a conference, he'll ask: *So, what are you finding of greatest value at the conference?* He always gets great answers and it leads him down a path of further questioning.

If you meet people who have changed industries, ask what prompted them to go from industry A to industry B; what they find similar between the industries and what they see as different. Think about their functional area. Is being in finance in a healthcare organization vastly different from being in finance for a public utility—both highly regulated industries? Find out why. Do they prefer one industry/company over another? Find out why.

If they're new to an industry, offer to connect them with someone you know from that industry. Perhaps they can glean some insights. If they've been in the industry for a while, offer to connect them with someone who is in a different industry, but performs a similar business function or operates a similar business model.

Ask what their current responsibilities and big initiatives are. *What are you working on these days?* is a pretty simple way to put it. Follow it up with, *How's it going? Any stumbling blocks? Like what?* Do you know anyone else who's dealing with these same initiatives? Offer to connect them.

Don't worry about prying. If people feel as if you're prying, they'll usually tell you. More times than not, though, when they say they don't want to talk about something, within five minutes, they open up and start talking about that very same thing.

One-on-one meetings

Meeting one-on-one is a great way to strengthen the foundation of your relationships with people.

Your goal in this meeting is threefold. You want to:

- Get to know them better.
- Figure out how you can help them.
- Identify others in their networks with whom you would like to build a relationship.

Start with thanking them for their time. Next, go into Molly's Top 7. Again, if you already asked those questions previously, it's probably best not to repeat yourself. If you've forgotten the answers, check their bio, LinkedIn profile, or any notes you took from previous interactions, before you meet.

Start with the big picture. *What's going on in the industry? What are the trends? What's changing? How are other influences driving change? How has the iPhone changed the way they do business? How has Facebook changed the way they reach more people? How has Amazon affected their business?* Oh, it hasn't yet? Give it time.

4.2

Continue with questions until you're done. Don't worry about not telling them your life story. You're not trying to make it about you. You're trying to ascertain who they know, who might be beneficial for you to meet, and to whom you can introduce them.

When they mention a company or contact you'd like to meet, ask for a referral right away. *Hey, I'd love to connect with Phil. Do you mind if I use your name?* Write it down. Getting a referral within the first few minutes of meeting someone takes all of the pressure off at the end. And you can turn one networking contact into many.

If they want to give you more time, take it. If you've run out of questions, it's time to wrap up. If you've identified future networking contacts throughout the meeting, hopefully you've already asked if you could reach out to them. If you've done a good job of engaging them in conversation, they will probably have a few contacts for you. If you haven't, and talked about yourself the entire time, you need to remember that showing up and throwing up rarely helps, and more often hinders, potential relationships.

One of my all-time favorite books is called *Competing for the Future* by Gary Hamel and C. K. Prahalad. They talk about market leadership and how market leaders of today are not always market leaders of tomorrow. Specifically, on page 18, they list questions that management should be asking to ensure they're reinventing themselves in order to remain competitive. If you think along the lines of Michael Porter's Five Forces of Industry Competition Model, and then think into the future, you'll start to create more leading questions.

4.2

Questions into the Future

Today	5 to 10 Years in the Future
Who are your customers today?	Which customers will you be serving in the future?
Who are your competitors today?	Who will be your competitors in the future?
What is the basis for your competitive advantage?	What will be the basis for your competitive advantage in the future?
What skills/capabilities make you unique today?	What skills or capabilities will make you unique in the future?

These are just a few, but pick up a copy of their book, and read page 18. Better yet, read the entire book. It will really get you thinking about market leadership, competition, reinvention, and innovation. People rarely have a chance to take time out of their busy day to sit back and wax eloquent on these topics. By providing that opportunity for them, they'll enjoy the interaction that much more.

Think about the *who, what, where, why, when* and *how.*

4.2

> *Who are your customers/buyers?*
>
> *Who is your competition?*
>
> *What are the trends in your industry?*
>
> *Where is your market opportunity coming from?*
>
> *What market forces are prompting change?*
>
> *When will you know that what you're doing is working? What are your key indicators of success?*
>
> *How are you going to reinvent yourself to compete effectively?*

SMART NETWORKING QUESTIONS

Here's how you put it into practice. Here's a conversation with Sharon, a grocery industry professional.

Start the conversation like this. *Sharon, thanks so much for taking the time to meet with me. I really appreciate it. Bill said if anyone knows about the food industry, it's you!*

Then, continue with questions, like this:

> *How long have you worked at [company]?*
>
> *And where were you before that? How long were you there?* Here, you're looking for other possible connections.
>
> *What are the biggest changes going on in the industry?*
>
> *Of all of the players, who do you think is best positioned for those changes? In particular, what are they doing that's different?*
>
> *What's changing in the way people shop for food?*
>
> *How does that differ within demographic circles?*
>
> *What's the next wave or trend that everyone is trying to implement?*
>
> *Which area of the store is most profitable? What's contributing to its profitability? Which areas of the store are least profitable? Why?*
>
> *Grocery stores are focused on the fourth wall. They are also banks, flower shops, DVD/video rentals, nail salons, medical clinics, coffee/ juice bars. It is just a leasing situation or some kind of revenue share? What's next?*
>
> *Which competitors do you think are going to lead the pack? Who's going to fall behind? What do you think are their options?*
>
> *How does grocery shopping differ among geographies? What about internationally?*

How big a threat is consolidation? Or do you think those companies will grow more by opening new formats? What about co-location and joint marketing opportunities?

How much do the food manufacturers play a role in the future of the store? How is category management affecting profits? Which categories and manufacturers are more progressive and innovative? What kind of things are they doing? How big a factor are coupons? What about coupon fraud? What kind of systems or processes are retailers and manufacturers putting in place to reduce fraud?

Where do you think you'll take the loyalty card program? From which industries (hotel, airline) are you taking lessons? What are you doing with the data? What would you like to do with the data?

How are the big box or hypermarkets' foray into grocery affecting your business? What about Amazon?

How are the niche players in the farmer's market/natural market concept affecting your business?

Who do you think your competition will be in the future —particularly those not currently competing with you today?

4.2

Keep in mind, I haven't really spent any time in the grocery industry, unless you count the three weeks in college where I worked for Lawry's & Lipton merchandising the shelves, refilling the taco seasoning tray, and dusting off the bottles of barbeque sauce. I quit after three weeks. It gave me headaches. It's giving me one right now just thinking about it.

I came up with these questions because I've been to a grocery store. I've purchased food. I pass by the Starbucks on my way into the store. I pass by the bank and video rental on my way out. I shop at more than one chain. I met someone on a plane who sold cookies to store bakeries. The trend at the time was inexpensive multi-packs—10 cookies for a dollar. They flew off the shelves. I met another person on the plane who sold high-end chocolate and gave me a primer on the geographic gourmet corridor—chocolate trends start on opposite coasts in the U.S., the Northeast and California—and move inland. I read an article about Tesco. And one about Walmart. And one on Target. I have some friends in the grocery business. I'm no expert when it comes to the industry, but I do know how to get people talking about this industry or any industry. Because it's all about asking smart questions, and actively listening to the answers. And I know it's more important to show what I know by the questions I ask than by the answers I give.

You have to give to get.

Throughout this discussion, if Sharon mentioned the name of a company doing innovative, interesting things, I asked right then and there if she knew someone at that company. *Great! I'd love to give them a call. Do you mind if I use your name?* If she gave me the okay, then I already had one contact with whom to follow up. I'd do this throughout the discussion. As I've said before, getting the names along the way removes all of the pressure of trying to secure contacts at the end.

More than getting names, though, I'm really focused on giving names. I'm constantly looking for ways to connect Sharon with other people in the industry, such as the high-end chocolate guy and another grocery expert in a different geography.

Smart questions lead to interesting conversations and insight into how you might be able to help others, which leads to other people opening up their networks to you. The more people you talk to and learn from, the better your questions are, the easier the connections come, and the more likely you'll be able to turn simple

4.2

networking meetings into something more valuable like really great relationships. Many of those same questions can apply to other industries by simply substituting a word or two.

Do not ask the person, *How can I help you?* People who ask this question as a general statement without some context around it have not done a good job of getting to know the other person. Throughout the discussion, look for opportunities where you can help them. Maybe they mentioned an initiative, and you know someone at another company/industry who is trying to implement the same initiative. Offer to connect the two. Perhaps they can learn from each other.

Take Mike, a chief information officer of a large insurance company, whom I met on the plane.

> Mike and I talk about his insurance company's customer service operation, and I ask if they are utilizing, or thinking about utilizing, at-home agents—customer service agents who work from their homes. Mike says, *Funny you should ask. I was just in a management meeting and we were talking about that very subject.* I tell him I know someone at JetBlue, a company that's been getting good press about its at-home agent program. Would his team be interested in speaking with the team over at JetBlue to gain some insight? He says he'd love it.
>
> I call John, my friend in JetBlue's training department, and ask him if he can connect me with the call center operations people who are responsible for the at-home agent program. He connects me with Chris. I explain to Chris that I am trying to help my friend at an insurance firm. Is she open to having a conversation with him about the at-home agent program? She says sure. A couple of weeks later, I call Mike to see if he

4.2

and Chris have had a chance to connect. Not only have they connected, his company is flying a team of people to JetBlue's offices for a half-day meeting to discuss the benefits and pitfalls of an at-home agent program.

Sure, it's been a little extra work for me. But what I've gotten out of it is the beginnings of a deeper relationship. If I ever need something from Mike, I'm sure he'd be glad to help me out!

Networking relationships that don't make it past go

Sometimes it happens. Not all relationships work out. When relationships are headed south—either internally or externally—go back to the vision. If things become confrontational, go back to the vision. If you're getting buried in the details and it doesn't look as if there's a way out, go back to the vision. What are you trying to accomplish overall? If you're headed down a path, and the person seems irritated, lighten it up.

Let's face it. You won't click with everybody. Some people will be easier than others to speak with. But if you focus on asking thoughtful questions, your opportunity to relate to people is greater.

4.2

When is it my turn?

In many of my training programs, attendees ask, *When is it my turn to speak? At what point do I get offended by the fact that they're showing no interest in me?* The answer? *Never.* This reminds me of the Biblical verse (Luke 12:48): *To those whom much is given, much will be required.* Or, as John F. Kennedy rephrased it, *To those whom much is given, much is expected.*

If you're more concerned that you've done all the asking, and perhaps it's time for the other person to show an interest in you, you're not getting it. You're not getting that you have to give in order to get. You have to seek first to understand. You have to care more about helping them than getting help. And it's then, and only then, that you start to become a great relationship builder.

Now that you are aware and in the know, much is expected of you. Honestly, life was easier when you didn't know this, when you didn't have to drive the conversation, when you didn't have to think about what to ask. But now that you are aware, it is your responsibility to keep the conversation moving. It is your responsibility to extract from others what you never knew. It is your responsibility to figure out how to help others before you ever think to ask for something for yourself. And if you're still bothered by the fact that most people barely know anything about you, just give it time. Give the relationship time to build and grow. You'll get your turn. As you grow your relationship the 100/0 will move more to something like 80/20—with them speaking 80% of the time, you speaking 20%. But that's okay. Because who do you know the most? Yes, you. And over time, how much more information do you need to know about yourself? That's right. None. So really, when you look at it that way, 20% is actually a huge amount of time!

4.2

The Networked Organization Action Plan

- Develop your set of smart questions.
- Show you're a good listener by taking good notes.
- Give, give, give before you ever think of getting.
- It is your responsibility to keep the conversation moving.
- Don't ask, *How can I help you?*

4.2

NETWORKING
FOLLOW-UP GUIDE

When to follow up

To be successful in networking you need to have perseverance. You need to be diligent. You need to close the loop. You need to follow up. This is easier said than done.

Have you ever walked out of an event or meeting without any follow-up? Okay, don't ever do that again. Always have some kind of follow-up. Always create an action item for yourself, preferably in the form of a connection. Always create a reason to continue the conversation. Always think about what value you can bring to the people you meet.

Is it ever too late to follow up?

You've just been to an event and met some great people or had a one-on-one. You get back to the office and have to handle some situations. A week goes by. Then another. Then another. Pretty soon, the interaction that produced some great contacts is more than a month ago. You think about following up, but a phone call comes in.

Then, whoops, it's time to go to that appointment. Next thing you know, two months have passed. By now, you've forgotten all of your action items anyway, and you're more than a little embarrassed. So, what do you do? Is it too late to follow up? Is it too unprofessional to ask the people you met if you owe them something?

Honestly, no and no. It's never too late to follow up. And it's okay to be human and say, *I think I owed you some follow-up, but I can't for the life of me remember what it was.*

Everybody is busy. Most people are not sitting around in life waiting for you to follow up with them.

How to follow up properly

A typical first follow-up action is to send a thank-you note. Should it be handwritten? Should it be in the form of an email? In this day and age, it probably doesn't matter. A handwritten thank you is great, but an email thank you is easier when it comes to addressing action items and creating a two-way communication.

I ran a workshop with high-potential employees of a major professional services firm. Over lunch, a panel of senior partners shared their experiences. When the panelists left, I had everyone take out a piece of paper and write a thank-you letter to one of the five panelists.

4.3

I read the thank-you letters aloud to the group. Many of them looked something like this:

> Dear Jason,
>
> Thank you for taking the time to meet with us. I was really impressed with your approach. I can see how clients would enjoy working with you. I learned a great deal from your advice.
>
> I look forward to learning more from you.
> Rebecca

Molly's Tip: This is not a Thank-You Letter

Here was another:

> Dear Kathy,
>
> I really appreciate the time you took out of your day to speak with us. I had no idea how much you focus on building the company brand.
>
> I would love to grab coffee with you when you are available.
>
> Thank you,
> Jonathan

Molly's Tip: This, too, is not a Thank-You Letter

Why not?

I, I, I, I. I this. I that. That's not a thank-*you* letter, it's a Thank-*I* letter. This is what a Thank-YOU letter looks like:

`4.3`

Molly's Thank-YOU Letter

> Dear Jason,
>
> Wow! What great advice you gave. It's no wonder you are one of the youngest people to make partner in the firm. Your dynamic and thoughtful approach creates such incredible relationships and results. Amazing!
>
> What was especially interesting was that story you told about how you built a relationship with the CEO of Conoco Phillips. Very creative!
>
> Perhaps we can meet up for coffee in the next week or two?
>
> Thank you,
> Rebecca

The concept of a Thank-YOU letter is making it all about them, and nothing about with you. Focus your statements on the person to whom you're writing. A good Thank-YOU letter never starts sentences with the word "I." It's exciting and enthusiastic with plenty of compliments and praise.

The next time you meet with someone, do the polite thing and send him or her a Thank-YOU letter. It won't guarantee you the business, but it might forge a stronger relationship.

4.3

After the Thank-YOU Letter, a good way to keep in contact—and therefore, on the person's mind—is to connect that person with someone interesting, email relevant articles, or provide a status of referrals, like, *Thanks so much for referring me to John. He seems great. We're meeting next week.* If you're having trouble connecting with the referral, this would be a good time to ask for help. Perhaps they could intervene and shoot off a quick email or voicemail requesting that person spend a few minutes with you.

Why do you want me to have you top of mind?

I may not be your customer, but I probably know your customer. Do you have any idea how many people I know? Do you know how many people I meet on a daily, weekly, and monthly basis? Let's just say it's a lot. And while all of these interactions aren't meant to turn into long-lasting relationships, on average I build more relationships in a month than most people do in a year. It's in your best interest for me to not only know you, but to like you.

Who in your network is like me? How can you stay on their radar?

What can you do to stay top of mind?

The people probably known the best for their keep-in-touch marketing campaigns are realtors. These are the same people probably known for the worst keep-in-touch programs. Right after them you'll find financial planners. Their idea of keeping in touch is sending out a monthly corporate email and customizing it by putting their name in the From line.

I may not be your **CUSTOMER,** but I probably know **YOUR CUSTOMER.**

Instead of keeping in touch, I'd recommend being in touch. Reach out to people, give them a call, check in to see what's up; actively look for ways to help them in the form of a lead, contact, or idea. That little phone call goes a long way, mostly because people don't do it anymore. Sure, you'll see plenty of updates on LinkedIn and Facebook, but something about getting together in person or, at a minimum, talking on the phone, takes the relationship to another level.

4.3

You want people to keep you top of mind. You want people to think of you. Think about the people you remember the best. The ones I remember are those who do interesting things. I also remember how funny they are or how much I enjoy myself when I'm around them. A great example of this is my friend Kris Calef who runs a monthly club business—beer of the month, wine of the month, cigar of the month, chocolate of the month, and more. It's called *monthlyclubs.com*. Kris is also one of the funniest and most genuine people I know. It's not often, but when I do come across a potential partnership for Kris, I feel good about it. I feel good because he's brought a lot of feeling good to a lot of people, especially with the beer and wine. Really, Kris is such a good person that I feel good helping him out in any way I can. I know that when I refer Kris, he'll bring an upbeat attitude to the conversation.

At the end of the day, when I refer someone, I want to ensure that it will be a positive interaction for all involved. I really have a hard time helping those who are negative, or those who show up in sweatpants. I'm afraid it will reflect poorly on me. On the other hand, being around someone who is very positive, professional, and great fun inspires me to do what I can to spread the joy.

Is it possible to be too exciting?

4.3

Some people are uncomfortable with the idea of being too exciting. Some people are uncomfortable with the idea of having too much enthusiasm. It's just not natural for some, and sometimes that discomfort really shows. But if you want people to refer you, you need to be positive. You need to be upbeat. You need to have energy. You need to smile. You need to be helpful. You need to figure out a way to help others. You need to show others that you are worthy of their referral, and that their friends will appreciate their referring you to them.

Networking Pitfall: Making assumptions about why someone hasn't responded

Let's say you contacted someone on Monday. It's now Wednesday and you're trying to figure out why that person is avoiding you. Here's a thought: It has nothing to do with you. That person is busy.

One of the worst things you can do is make assumptions about why someone hasn't responded to your influx of calls and emails.

I had a situation where someone contacted me for a referral. He left a message. I was out of town. Three days later, he left another message. I was still out of town. Two days after that, he sent me an email saying, *I thought you were going to help me, but I guess I was mistaken*. Actually, I *was* going to help him, but I'm not now. If he's uptight about my not calling back when I'm busy, what's he going to do to someone I refer him to? This was years ago. And you know what? My life is no less fulfilled by him not being in it. Maybe his life isn't either without me being in it. But I can tell you that he missed out on a really great referral.

Another person I know, we'll call him Tad, was trying to get in touch with Greg. A couple weeks passed and I asked Tad if he'd been able to connect with Greg. *Oh, he finally called me back*, said Tad. Sensing there was more to the story, I asked Tad what he'd done to elicit the magical response. *I left Greg yet another message*, he said, *and told him it was "improper not to respond."*

Well, congratulations, Tad, you've won the battle and lost the war. Greg may have gotten back to you, but with that attitude, there's no way he's going to help you today, tomorrow, or ever. He simply returned your call, checked off the box, and never has to talk to you again. However, your conversation will likely have some lingering

4.3

effects. In fact, if there's ever an interaction between Greg and someone who brings up your name, I'm guessing Greg might suggest that you might be more than a tad annoying.

We all fall into traps occasionally, and even the best intentions can go awry. A few years back, I had an opportunity to work with one of IBM's partner organizations. I'd done a lot of work with IBM, but none with this group. I was introduced to the decision maker. I met with her that very same day. We really hit it off and I was looking forward to the next conversation. We talked one more time on the phone about my presenting at one of their conferences. I followed up. No response. I followed up again. No response. The conference was fast approaching and I was getting worried. Had they already booked their lineup of speakers? With just 45 days out, I didn't know what to do. I left the sorriest voicemail ever. I never heard back. It was so sorry that I'm not sure I would've called me back either. Someday, maybe I'll be a speaker for one of their conferences, but I was so focused on the impending event that I lost the entire opportunity. It's situations like this that remind me there's always another time, another day, another year. Exercising self-control is not always easy, is it?

Following up without being a pest can be difficult. If you're so focused on people's responding, then give them a good reason to respond. Don't forget, everyone has a lot going on. They can have great intentions, but other priorities in life can take precedence. Have some patience. Cut people some slack. To pass the time, why don't you get busy and follow up with other people on your list, or identify and contact others with whom you want to pursue a relationship?

The Networked Organization Action Plan

- It's never too late to follow up.

- Perfect the art of the Thank-YOU letter.

- Be sure your interactions are positive ones for all involved.

- Never make assumptions about why someone hasn't responded.

- Relationships are not built in a day, but over a lifetime.

4.3

NETWORKING ETIQUETTE

I said it earlier: When technology walks in, manners seem to walk out. While we all have our own way of doing things, here is some general etiquette that might make your networking efforts go more smoothly.

Meeting etiquette

I take all my notes on my computer. Okay, good for you. No doubt you're helping the environment, but you're not doing much to help your relationships. Here's what I'm thinking when you're taking notes on your laptop while you're in a one-on-one/face-to-face conversation with me: *Hmm, I wonder if he's checking his email. I wonder if he's checking out the scores of yesterday's football games. I wonder if he's looking at the weather. I wonder if he's planning his next vacation. Yes, that's definitely it.* I pretty much assume you're doing anything but actually taking notes on your conversation with me.

The problem with taking notes on a computer when someone is talking to you is that it could be perceived as rude. Even if you have positive intent and all you're truly doing is taking notes, most people don't believe that's the case. It's your choice. Next time you decide to take notes on a computer in front of someone, think real hard about whether breaking out a pen and piece of paper might be worth it for the sake of the relationship.

Put the phone away. In a one-on-one/face-to-face meeting, having your phone in sight or looking at your phone while someone is talking to you is not polite. If you're looking something up on your phone for that person, let them know what you're doing and why you're doing it. If you constantly check your phone for email or texts out of habit, put the phone away where you can't see it, feel it, or hear it. If you're worried that by putting your phone out of reach you'll forget it, place it with your car keys. If you've scheduled a meeting with someone and a family member went into the hospital that morning, let them know. *Hey, we had a family emergency this morning. If I get a call from one of my family members while we're meeting, I'm going to have to step out and take it, but I'll make it quick.* Otherwise, if the phone rings while you're in a meeting, let it ring. Nothing's worse than meeting with someone who, when their phone rings, looks at it and says, *I don't know who this is,* and then proceeds to answer it.

4.4

Take back control of your own life. Let voicemail get it.

The use of email

Email should be used for confirming appointments and following up. Not for conversations. This reminds me of a friend I call Tidal Wave Dave. Tidal Wave Dave comes at you whether you want him to or not. His emails are the equivalent of a 17-page monologue. Nobody wants to read a two-page email, let alone a 17-page one.

Not receiving responses from your emails? Perhaps you're writing them in a way that makes people want to delete them after the first sentence. Here are some of my basic email tenets:

- An email should take up no more than one screen. No one should have to page down during an email. If it's longer than that, you need to preface it by putting FYI (for your information) at the top and expect people to assume it's leisure reading. If it's more important than leisure reading, pick up the phone or schedule a meeting to discuss the items.

- Action items should be listed in the first sentence. Want to meet someone for coffee? Let them know in the first sentence. Want to get confirmation for your meeting? Request confirmation in the first sentence.

- If you have more than one subject in your email, label them with categories or headings. If you have multiple items in each category, bullet or number the items.

- Did you carbon copy the entire world on your email? Was it really necessary? Did you cc: anyone's boss? Do you know what extra work you're now putting that person through? Was that your intention?

Make it easy for people to respond to you. Make emails short, sweet, and to the point.

Your email signature line

Last week, I received an email from Jerri, someone with whom we're doing business. Jerri had some bad news to share so she emailed me. When I picked up the phone to call her about it, I realized her phone number wasn't in the email. I went to another email she sent me and looked for her number. It wasn't there either. I went through all of the emails Jerri had sent me in the past two months. Not one of them had her phone number. Not one of them had a signature line. That's when I began to get frustrated. It's bad enough that she sent me an email to deliver bad news instead of calling me, but she made it even worse by making it difficult to call her back.

I finally googled the number at Jerri's company. By then, my frustration with the email was coupled with my frustration at wasting time trying to track her down.

About an hour later, I needed to get a hold of Jim, a business associate. I went into my email to find his number. He didn't have his phone number or a signature line in his email either.

Later that day, I was trying to introduce two people to each other. I had emails from both, but neither—that's right, neither—had email addresses in their signature line. Sometimes Outlook only shows the name in the From line, not the person's email address. This means I have to take the extra steps of locating the email and adding the name to the rest of the contact information before I can paste that contact information into a new introduction email.

That's when I thought, *Is this a conspiracy? Is the world out to get me? Does no one realize the value of putting detailed contact information into a signature line to save others time?*

In this world of high-speed communications, you need to do your part to keep the concept of *high speed* in high speed. You need to make it easy for people to reach you. You need to make it easy for people to refer you.

4.4

I think the problem is that most people have their signature line set up on their company email, but the majority of issues lie in the Reply To feature. Most people don't include their signature line again in the replies. It's time you did. Please, make it easy for everyone else. Remember the Golden Rule of Networking: *Networking is not about you.* It's about everyone but you.

What can you do to make it about everyone but you? Fix your signature line and Reply To signature right now. Here's what you want in your work email signature line: name, company, email, phone number, and website. In your personal one, put your name, email, and phone number.

Please, save the rest of us a little time and a lot of frustration.

Finally, remember that email is no way to deliver bad news. Pick up the phone, people!

While I'm at it, let me mention a few other things regarding email that you ought to consider.

The From line. The From line shows me who the email is from before I ever look at it. The other day, I received an email from *Con Man*. It stood for Consultant Manager, but honestly how can I refer someone with a From line like that? *I'd like to introduce you to Con Man. You're welcome!*

Don't let your lack of personal branding knock you out of the professional game. And if you think it won't…guess what? It probably already did.

How to answer your phone

You might think you already know how to answer your phone. After all, you've probably been doing it quite a while. But let me challenge you to think hard about it. Are you answering in a voice that says *I'm glad you called,* or do you act as if every call is an interruption of your crazy, busy, fantastic, no-time-for-anyone-else life? Think about the tone of voice you use in your greeting. And don't just say hello. Let them know whom they've reached. Here's a hot tip, put a mirror at

4.4

your desk and look at it while you're on the phone. It will help you remember to smile. People can hear when you're smiling. People can hear when you're not smiling.

Growing up, my parent's friends liked calling our house because all of the kids in my family were trained to answer the phone like this: *Hello. Wendell Residence, [name] speaking.* People knew that they had the correct number and, more importantly, knew to whom they were speaking. It drives me crazy when I call my sister Mary's house and one of her many children answers the phone. The boys sound like girls and I always end up calling Michael one of his sisters, Lucy or Emma. Finally, I decided to start with Michael so as to no longer offend him. It would be a lot easier for me if they'd answer the phone the way we did as kids. Again, networking is not about you, it's about everyone else but you. Even when you're five.

And while we're on the subject of answering phones, think about where you answer your cell phone. If you're like most people, you answer it anywhere and everywhere, like that woman in the restroom the other day. I think that was one call that could have waited. If you're in a meeting, do not answer your cell phone. If you are in the middle of a big project deadline, do not answer your cell phone. If the next sentence out of your mouth is about to be, *This isn't a good time,* do not answer your cell phone.

4.4

And don't forget about phone greetings: You need to have one. Have you ever been on the other end of a computer voice that says *You've reached 508-6782?* Did you think, even for a split second, that you might have dialed the wrong number? Do you wonder if you're leaving a message for someone you don't know? Do everyone else a favor, please personalize your voicemail. Give them confirmation they've actually reached you and not some stranger.

Be straightforward.

Nobody likes mystery when it comes to answering your phone. Nothing makes me more suspicious than the phone call that goes something like this: *Hello Molly, a friend of yours gave me your name and suggested we meet.*

My first thought is that this person is trying to pitch me on some multi-level marketing scheme. Again, remember the advice from my sixth-grade English teacher: *To be specific is terrific. To be vague is the plague.*

As I said, whenever the phone rings, most busy people are thinking, *Who are you and why are you wasting my time?* Therefore, it's critical to state your name, purpose, and your referral source up front. If it's a good purpose, or better yet, a good referral, you might buy a few more seconds of their time.

Remember Molly's renowned call/call/email approach?

> "Hi [Bill,] this is Molly Wendell. [Carol McDaid] suggested I give you a call to set up a time to meet. I'm new to the [aerospace] industry and [Carol] said if there's anyone who could give me insight into the industry, it's you. I'm really looking forward to meeting. I can be reached at 312-123-4567. Again, my number is 312-123-4567. Thank you."

4.4

Quit calling people Mr., Mrs., or Ms.

After you've graduated from college, the only appropriate time to address someone with the title Mr., Mrs., or Ms. is when you're meeting your parents' friends or the head of a country. And in the latter case, you'd use the title of president, prime minister, king/

queen, raj, emperor/empress, or whatever the rest of their country calls them. And, if you're hanging out in those circles, I really hope you are reading this.

Quit addressing people through email, letter, or in person by anything other than their first name. And that goes for *Dear Sir or Madam*. What, are we still in the eighteenth century?

Some people say addressing others with such formality is a sign of respect. I might suggest that it's awkward, and even more awkward when you get it wrong. Have you ever used the title Mrs. when speaking to an unmarried woman? Or worse, called her Mrs. Smith—only to find out it's her maiden name—and, hold on just a minute, she'll have to see if her mother is available to meet with you. Have you ever assigned the wrong gender to Chris, Pat, Terry, Shannon, Leslie, Jamie, or Lynn?

The most appropriate way to show someone a sign of respect is to call them by their name. It puts you both on a level playing field. Show them you know how to be an adult who is worthy of an actual conversation.

How to introduce a speaker

Have you ever been to an event where the person introducing the speaker says, *This speaker needs no introduction?* Well, that person is lazy and a liar. Everyone needs an introduction. Not only do you need an introduction, you deserve an introduction. A thoughtful introduction. It doesn't matter who you are.

A good introduction helps pave the way for you. It establishes credibility with the audience. It gives you a thumbs up before you ever go on stage. It says, *This person is great and you're going to enjoy listening to him/her for these reasons.*

4.4

A professional speaker once told me that he quit giving a bio to his clients because they actually read it. In front of everyone. Word for word. And that 11-sentence bio started to feel like 10 too many.

The best introductions captivate the audience and prepare them for the speaker. Some of the best introductions I've heard included a short, personal story about how the introducer and speaker met, or talked about something they'd been discussing. Thoughtful introductions include things that the speaker may not say about him or herself.

I once attended an event where the person introducing the speaker spoke for so long that when the speaker got up he said, *We should probably wrap it up. Thanks for your time. Any questions?*

Next time you have the incredible opportunity to introduce someone, be thoughtful about it. Look for ways to compliment the speaker. Look for ways to make it personal. Look for ways to make it interesting. And, above all, look for ways to make it brief.

Your intro might sound something like this:

> "The first time I met Molly, she shook my hand and just said, 'Uh, we'll work on that.' Since then, I've learned that a great handshake is only the beginning when it comes to building great relationships. It's the little things, all combined, that make up that first great, lasting impression.

4.4

> "Molly has been featured as a networking expert on all the major news stations, ABC, NBC, CBS, Fox and WGN. You're in for a real treat because she is not only going to refine our handshake, but give us the tools to leverage that first great impression into building truly lasting relationships. Please welcome Molly Wendell!"

Invite people to coffee, not lunch.

Why is inviting people to lunch poor networking etiquette? I mean, who doesn't like lunch? My sister Katy loves lunch. I like lunch, too, but I don't know if I like you yet. The thought of meeting you for the first time over what may be the longest lunch ever? I'll take a pass.

I am, however, glad to meet you for coffee. I will budget 45 minutes to an hour. I don't even drink coffee, but that's beside the point. I want to meet you at Starbucks. Some of you might say that it's very noisy, but I say go where the people go. If I meet you at a Starbucks close to your office, someone you know may stop in. And now I've just gotten a possible bonus connection.

Say someone has agreed to go to lunch with you. That's great. Just remember, meals require a greater time commitment. What if you realize after 15 minutes that you're really not connecting with this person? Getting up from the table and walking out is not always the smoothest departure. Trust me, I've thought about it. Plus, figuring out who's paying can sometimes be a little uncomfortable. Should I pay? Are you going to pay? Do we split it? It's a scenario that can be avoided by not going to lunch in the first place.

Here's a hasty generalization. Men like breakfast. I'm not sure if it's because they never get a home-cooked breakfast anymore, or that they want to shirk all family responsibility for getting the kids ready for school. *Sorry, honey. I'd love to help you out, but I have a breakfast meeting. Got to run.* It's probably because there's less of a chance of their schedule going awry compared to later in the day. Either way, in much of my networking, I've found that men suggest breakfast. I don't enjoy eating breakfast out, so I usually move it to coffee. It doesn't make them want to meet with me any less.

4.4

If you suggest coffee and they suggest breakfast or lunch, you can certainly take it. Just know what decision points you have to deal with.

Being prepared

Nothing's worse than heading into a networking meeting without doing some sort of prep work.

> I have a meeting with David. I walk into his office and see a rather sizable aquarium. Fortunately, I've done my research and know that David is a huge fan of fish and the aquarium concept. He belongs to some aquarium groups and regularly contributes to their online discussions.
>
> If I hadn't known this, I probably would've walked in, seen the aquarium, and started into a diatribe of how I think aquariums and pet fish are the biggest waste of time and money ever. I mean, what's interesting about staring at a fish in a murky container? Oh, look, its gills opened. Oh, now it went under that rock. *Want to watch me feed it?* No, I don't, as a matter of fact. What I'd prefer is to watch you not feed it. Try that for many days in a row…and then see what happens. Maybe then you'll clean that thing. It's disgusting and it smells.
>
> The meeting could be a catastrophe, but I've done my research. I refrain and don't dare go anywhere near the whole fish topic, because I know that doing so won't leave David with a positive impression of me.

Hopefully you've done some research to uncover more about the person you're going to meet to identify some common bonds and

4.4

avert potential disasters. At least do the basic things like Google the person, read a bio, find out what community or charity events they support. There's a fine line between stalking and being prepared.

When you meet with the person armed with so much knowledge about them, there's no need to divulge it all. Little things can be dropped into the conversation very casually. I remember sitting in a job interview with Dana a few years back. Prior to our meeting, I read her bio and saw that she was involved in a charity called Logopedics. Never heard of it? I'm not surprised. In fact, very few have heard of it other than those women who were in the college sorority of Kappa Alpha Theta. I checked the Alumna directory. Sure enough, there was her name.

The first thing I said when we met was, *Guess where I was this weekend?* Given that we'd never even met before, naturally Dana had no idea. *I went to Grand Convention,* I said. *Can you believe it?* I didn't even mention the word Theta because I knew she'd know. *No, no, I can't believe it,* she said. I think what she couldn't believe was the fact that I knew she was a Theta Alum. I told her a little about the convention, and how impressed I was with the women I'd met. Then, I asked her about her involvement in the local chapter. We had a great conversation, which actually turned into a job offer to be her boss, essentially.

4.4

I didn't need to tell Dana how I knew. I didn't need to go into detail about the research. I just put it out there, talked about it for a minute, and then moved on.

Another time, I was doing a networking training class for a professional services firm. In my preparation, I tried to learn a little something about each of the participants. I was showing how easy it was to learn about a person with a little online research. *Somebody is heavily involved in working with foster children, right*

Greg? A big congratulations to the person who just ran a marathon! Way to go, Sarah. I then asked, *Who has an anniversary coming up?* The room was silent. *No one has an anniversary coming up? No one?* Finally, I said, *Meghan, how about you? Do you have an anniversary next week?* Meghan gave me a blank stare. It took about 10 seconds, but then she said, *Oh (expletive), I do! Thanks for the reminder. How did you know?* How did I know? In my research, I'd stumbled upon a small-town newsletter that had printed information about her wedding a year ago.

Finding information about people is easy. Thank you, internet!

What I like better than finding activities is finding people we both know. Checking LinkedIn to find common connections is probably the easiest way—assuming both of your LinkedIn connections are authentic. But there are plenty of other ways. Is the person a coach on a little league baseball team? Look at the team roster and figure out if you know any other parents. Is the person on the board of a charity? Check the rest of the board to see if you know anyone on it. Where did the person used to work? Do you know anyone at that company? Where do they live? Maybe you know some of their neighbors. What about college? Maybe you know some of their classmates. Again, being prepared is not the same as stalking. It's a fine line, but a real one.

You'll be amazed what you find if you just do a little research. And you'll be even more amazed at how you can turn a good meeting into a great one simply by taking the time to find out a little about that person and how much he loves pet fish.

The Networked Organization Action Plan

- Take notes old school style—with a pen and paper.
- In your emails, put action items in the first line.
- Make sure the signature and Reply To line in your email has the same contact information as your business card.
- Personalize your phone greeting.
- Think about how you introduce people; make it personal and relevant.
- Do your research.

4.4

4.5

THE 7 ESSENTIAL
SECRETS OF SMART
NETWORKERS

Are you on the chopping block?

Have you ever watched the competitive cooking television show *Chopped*? In each episode, four chefs compete round by round to see who can cook the best dish in the time allotted using a basket of ingredients they're supplied along with other items available to them from the stocked pantry. At the end of each round, the chef with the dish judged the worst is *chopped*. In one episode, just as one of the chefs was in the last 30 seconds of making his main course, he realized he didn't have a sauce. After running to the pantry for some champagne vinaigrette, he settled instead on white truffle oil.

WHHHAAAATTTT???? Had he never seen the show prior to going on? Doesn't he know that white truffle oil is the kiss of death? Everybody who uses white truffle oil gets chopped. Everybody.

This poor chef's rookie mistake made me think of all the things I see when I'm networking. There's much more to meeting and greeting than people realize, which is probably why I see so many mistakes. Take the introduction, for instance. Most people introduce themselves in a way that is not at all inviting, enticing, or interesting. And by interesting, I don't mean some cutesy, contrived slogan.

The introduction

> Ted seems nice. Serious, but nice. He introduces himself and starts to tell me what he does for a living. That's great. I want to learn about him. But about five minutes in, as he continues to talk and talk and talk, I'm now wondering how he ever landed a customer-facing role. How could anyone at the company think that he would be a good fit to leave the four walls of his office and have real live interactions with other human beings? Then I find out he's one of the partners. Oh, that explains it. Ted bought his way into a customer-facing role.

What could Ted have done differently to make this interaction more palatable?

- Ted could've smiled. Why did he need to make talking to people seem like such a chore?
- Ted could've had some inflection and enthusiasm in his voice. Not everyone needs to be super outgoing, but a monotone delivery is a mortal blow when you're making conversation.
- Ted could've quit talking about himself. Some people need to learn when enough is enough. If you've been talking with, or rather at, someone for longer than 60 seconds, it's time for you to stop, take a breath, ask the other person a question and give them a chance to speak.

4.5

A low level of enthusiasm and monopolizing the conversation are probably the biggest mistakes I see, but many more are out there. And, they can undermine your ability to be successful in your relationship-building efforts.

If you really don't want to be inviting, enticing, or interesting, that's fine. Just quit coming to networking events and boring us to death. Because what we really want to do is *chop* you from the conversation. Not smiling enough? Chopped. No inflection in your voice? Chopped. Conversation not interesting? Chopped. Making rookie mistakes? Chopped. Oh, and using white truffle oil? Chopped!

Molly's Essential Secret #1

Smart Networkers don't hang out with people they already know.

There's one thing my husband knows to do when we're at a social or networking event together: Stay away from me. Far, far away. I do my best to stay away from him, too. Why? Because we both know the value of nurturing on-going relationships and forging new ones. Sure, we check in with each other periodically, but the whole reason we went to the event was to further relationships with *other* people. If you attend functions with friends or colleagues, you can simply point out your colleagues to people you meet and suggest they make an effort to introduce themselves. If you work together as a team, three of you could easily make nine new connections, three proactively and six reactively.

4.5

| Molly's Essential Secret #2

Smart Networkers don't make assumptions about other people's networks.

Too often, we make judgments about other people's networks. We decide whether their networks will or won't be valuable without even giving them a chance to see if there might be good connections through these relationships.

> I don't know if your network has two people, 200, or 2,000.
> ## IT'S MY JOB TO FIGURE IT OUT.

Whenever I'm meeting someone for the first time, I think about the guy in the old Verizon commercial—the one with the whole network of people behind him. I'm reminded that we all have a network behind us. I don't know if your network has two people, 200 or 2,000, but it's my job to figure it out.

> I'm on a flight from Orlando and sit next to an elderly gentleman. My first assumption when I meet him is that he is retired. After all, we're flying from Florida. But my assumption turns out to be wrong. Very wrong. This man, chairman of one of the largest companies in Denver, is actively involved in the organization. When I find out this man doesn't have a ride from the airport to his office, I offer to give him one, and he takes me up on it. He probably could call someone or even take a taxi, but I'm glad to do a favor for him. And who knows where our relationship might lead?

4.5

Sometimes it's not as obvious how to help people whose network already reads like a *Who's Who*. Sometimes it is. Often, we're too caught up in our own business to take the time to think about what we can do to build new relationships. Then when we need them, we don't have them. Again, I may not be your customer, but I may know your customer. And I may know others who know your customer, too.

I was presenting to a group about the idea that since you never know who people know it's best not to pre-judge. Someone in the audience raised his hand. *Yes, I get that,* he said, *but I'm not going to sit here and network with the cook at the restaurant. Who will he know?*

Good question, I said. *Let's talk about that. I have a nephew named Anthony. Anthony is a cook in a restaurant. And who does Anthony know?* The crowd yelled, *You, Molly.*

And who do I know? The crowd chimed in, *Everybody!*

So there you go. Always make friends with the cooks.

Next time you have the opportunity to be around people, which basically means next time you leave your home, leverage it. Make conversation with people, even perfect strangers. Focus on building relationships without preconceived notions of who knows whom. Get better at realizing that your next customer, board member, partner, co-worker or friend just might be seated next to you. And they're there for a reason.

Molly's Essential Secret #3

Smart Networkers don't ask, How can I help you?

Many professionals who consider themselves experts in the field of networking advise people to always end a networking meeting by saying *How can I help you?* I know how you can help me. You can start by never using that phrase again. People who ask this question as a general statement have not done a good job of listening, of getting to know the other person.

Honestly, it's not my job to figure out how you can help me. It's your job to figure it out. If you ask question after question and identify an opportunity to help someone, let them know, right then and there. You might even say *In addition to [identified way to help], are there any other ways you think I might be able to help you?* If you've asked question after question and haven't been able to figure out how to help someone, maybe you can't help them right now. Maybe you can't help them ever. Maybe that's okay. But if you really want to help someone, remember that it's your job to figure out how. Not theirs.

Molly's Essential Secret #4

Smart Networkers don't make it all about themselves.

Do your part to not make it about you. Most of my conversations consist of me asking questions and the other person answering them. I don't mind because I adhere to the Golden Rule of Networking: *It's not about you.* I know it's not about me. In fact, it's about everybody but me. And most of the time, when I adhere to this rule, I find that it's time well spent and I've laid the groundwork for a new relationship.

4.5

Those who don't adhere to practicing this Secret, be warned. Just because you're out there doesn't mean that you're necessarily making a good impression. A few years ago, I reached out to Mitchell.

Mitchell runs a big organization and I think it'll be good to meet each other. We set up a time for lunch. I think it'll be about an hour. Most busy people don't really have time for much more than that. My mistake is that I assumed Mitchell was busy. I thought he was interesting. I also thought he knew how to network. Wrong on all accounts. Three hours later, I am finally set free from what has been the most painful lunch I've ever experienced. And here's the crazy part. As we're leaving, he says, *This was so great. I had so much fun. We really ought to do it again!*

Were we at the same table? Did he experience the same lunch? Did someone spike his iced-tea? The only time we'll be having lunch again is…well, never.

Fortunately, this type of situation is rare. Most people are actually pretty interesting and I do enjoy getting to know them. But someone like Mitchell—who did the proverbial show up and throw up—is a problem. Don't be like Mitchell.

Be on the lookout for these signs:

- If you're dominating the conversation, you need to stop. That's not good networking.
- If you're telling story after story with no interaction among the rest of the parties, you need to stop. That's not good networking.
- If you walk away not knowing much about the person you just met, then you probably did too much talking and not enough listening. That's not good networking.

So, what do you do when someone is really good at engaging you? How do you know if others are enjoying the conversation as much as you are? How do you know if they even like you?

4.5

Sometimes it's pretty easy to tell. If you're both getting a good laugh out of the conversation and genuinely having a good time, it's a good sign. Sometimes, though, it's hard to tell. I would say, as a general rule, the answer lies in the follow up. Do they reach out to you unsolicited? When you reach out to them, are they available? Do they respond? I know I've really engaged someone when they follow up with me before I've had a chance to follow up with them. It happens more often than not.

Lack of response, though, isn't always an indicator. As we all know, sometimes people are busy. Sometimes emails get lost. Sometimes messages are taken but are then misplaced. If you call someone up and they seem genuinely surprised and excited to hear from you, it's probably safe to say that you've engaged them and they like you.

Molly's Essential Secret #5

Smart Networkers don't forget to follow up.

You want to know what's real easy? Not following up. Yes, it's really easy to not follow up. It takes no time or effort whatsoever. Next to not lifting a finger, it's just about the easiest thing in the world. On the other hand, following up takes time and effort, and we don't always have the time or the energy. But if you want to be great at building relationships, you need to be disciplined about following up. You need to deliver on your commitments to people. If you tell someone you're going to send her a copy of an article, then send it. If you tell her you're going to connect her with someone, then connect them. If you tell her you'll be in touch to set up coffee, get out your calendar.

Let's say some time has passed and you feel like it's too late to follow up. Do it anyway. You can be embarrassed. You can apologize. However, most people aren't waiting around in life for your follow up. It's never too late to follow up.

The more involved you are in networking, the more follow up you have to do. For every hour you spend networking, you probably have at least 20 minutes of follow up. A three-hour event is going to set you back an additional hour. Plan on it. Plan for it.

Molly's Essential Secret #6

Smart Networkers don't make inaccurate assumptions about the value of job seekers.

Be careful of pre-judging people. Many people shun those who are unemployed because they don't believe the unemployed can provide them value, or have the mindset that if those unemployed were any good, they'd have a job. Helping people who are in the job search is not only good for the job seeker, it's good for you, too.

What value do unemployed people bring? The big answer is market knowledge. While most employed people are too busy to do much of anything other than their jobs, people in the job search who are networking tend to meet a lot of people and hear what's going on around town. They could be an incredible resource to you for market information, mergers, acquisitions and growth.

How would you like your very own personal industry researcher? One job seeker I know who's trying to penetrate a new industry has done so much reading about the industry that he's gotten in the

4.5

289

habit of providing top-notch market reports to those already in the industry. These are people who, quite frankly, don't have the time to stay abreast of everything going on and are extremely appreciative.

Most unemployed people don't know how to perform an effective job search. They call and email everyone they've ever known, give them their *out of work but it was not my fault* story, attach their resume, and ask if they know anyone who is hiring. What value does this person bring? Not much. These job seekers need to read my book, *The New Job Search*!

Meeting a job seeker at a networking event, however, is a completely different story because this job seeker is actually out there meeting new people and building relationships. Some of those relationships could be of benefit to you.

Do you know what it's like to be unemployed, attend a networking event, and have no one talk to you because you're unemployed? Honestly, it's not fun, but it's a reality.

Next time you're at an event and meet a job seeker, here are a few things to think about instead of thinking how quickly you can give them the brush-off.

1. If you help people in their job search, they're typically thankful, and will likely go out of their way to help you. When you lend a hand to someone in need, that person won't soon forget who was gracious when they were down. When I was in a longer-than-expected job search, some of the best guidance I received was from a group of people I barely knew. They were much more helpful than my friends, family and past co-workers. These people were there when I was down. They were there when times were tough. And they did everything in their power to help me. To this day, I absolutely go out of my way to help them in any way I can.

4.5

2. *When you give someone in a job search some hope in the form of a lead or an idea, you stand out. You stand out from the many who don't give them the time of day. One day, when you're in that same position, they'll find ways to reciprocate. And don't think you won't be, because, trust me, most everyone in a job search never thinks it will happen to them.*

3. Again, while you're too busy to learn about what's going on in the rest of the world, that's exactly what these people are doing. Go to a networking meeting for those in the job search and you'll learn so much about what's going on in the local market in a very short time. Far less time than it would take you doing research on your own.

Most importantly, helping people is simply a nice thing to do. If you're like most people, you get a sense of joy from helping others. Remember that every person you meet who is in the job search is a father, mother, brother, sister, son or daughter. Wouldn't you want someone to be nice and help your family member, too?

And if you really want to help them out, don't forget to recommend my book, *The New Job Search*!

Molly's Essential Secret #7

Smart Networkers don't walk around with a frown.

4.5

It takes a lot of little impressions to make a big impression. It's with this in mind that I think about the idea of approachability.

It's hard to build relationships when people feel as if they can't talk to you. Have you ever said hello to someone only to have him practically bite your head off? Geez, pal, maybe you should lay off the caffeine for a while!

This idea of approachability is on my mind a lot. Too many times, I run across people who don't seem very approachable. And this is before I've even had the opportunity to meet them. What's my first clue? It's the face. It's the way they make, or don't make, eye contact. And it's the smile. It all comes down to the smile.

Why is smiling important? Because if you want to build relationships, you need to have a welcoming demeanor. One that says, *Hey, I'm someone to get to know. And I won't bite your head off.*

Some people walk around with a smile. My hasty generalization is that they lead a more positive life. I've also seen just the opposite—those who rarely smile. My hasty generalization here is that they're not as positive.

Which one are you? Which one do you want to be?

Do you want to have a more welcoming demeanor? Let me tell you, it's a lot easier to build relationships with one than without one. What can you do to develop yours more fully? Here are a few ideas:

1. Walk around making eye contact with others (not in a creepy way). Don't look away when someone looks at you. Break into a smile and say hello, good morning, or good afternoon.

2. When walking into the office, a meeting or a networking event, put your best face on. Say words to yourself like *cheese, bees,* (help me) *please.* They all end in a nice, pleasant smile. In other words, make yourself appear approachable.

3. Have a mentality that says *I'm here to help.* When you truly are here to help, people notice. Look for ways to offer a hand.

A few years ago, I saw a woman with her young daughter in a grocery store parking lot. She was crying so I asked her if she was okay. Turns out, she'd locked her keys in her car and her infant was still in the back seat. Tears streamed down as she told me that there was no way to open the car. Fortunately, I had owned the same model car and locked my keys in it one too many times. I retrieved my trusty coat hanger out of my trunk and went to work on the door lock. Within about 30 seconds, the door was open. The woman thanked me sincerely and whispered something to her little girl. As I was walking away, I heard her little girl ask, "Mommy, what's a savior?" I felt pretty good that day. If you look for ways to help out, not only will you feel good, but it generally comes back around.

There's plenty more when it comes to impressions, but approachability is a good starting point because if no one wants to approach you, it's pretty difficult to start, let alone build, deep relationships.

Molly's Bonus Essential Secret

Smart Networkers don't forget that a referral is always better than a cold call.

I learned this Essential Secret by not following my own advice when time was of the essence and I felt I couldn't afford to wait a moment longer. What a mistake! It went something like this:

> I want to get a meeting with Marty, a senior vice president of a fairly large technology company that shall remain nameless. Safe to say the company is the backbone of technology networks, and the name might rhyme with disco. I have this great idea that I'm sure will help them increase their business dramatically and I want to see if they're interested in some growth.

4.5

293

I'm on the internet Tuesday night and happen to notice the company is having a partner conference in my city on Thursday. Guess who the keynote speaker is? That's right. Marty! He and I will be in the same zip code. I have to take advantage of this incredible opportunity!

Quickly, I reach out to a few people who might know Marty. No response. So, I give Marty a heads-up. I leave a message on his voicemail Wednesday night letting him know I'll drop by the conference, match a name with a face, and say hello. No warm intro. No one to vouch for me. Just an enthusiastic voicemail letting him know I just want a minute of his time.

Thursday comes along, and I'm ready. I look very professional, and no one in their right mind will confuse me for the absolute stalker I am apparently about to become. I'm a bit nervous. I can't recall the last time I approached someone without a warm introduction. I think it was Steve Jobs back in the mid-1990s. This is going to work out really well, as it had with Steve, or really poorly.

I get to the hotel conference center 20 minutes before Marty is scheduled to finish his speech. Immediately I'm stopped by a large man named Richard. *You need to get a badge,* he tells me. No problem. I can do that. I waltz over to the registration desk and explain my situation. *I'm here to see Marty. I need to quickly get a badge before he finishes speaking so I can catch him before he leaves town.* Felicity, my new best friend at the conference registration desk, can't seem to get in touch with anyone on the team who can authorize me to walk in the door. Richard keeps glaring at me from afar. Somehow I've got to get out from under his watch.

Now I have only 10 minutes before Marty is going to finish. I'm not sure which way he'll exit. I decide to make sure he won't escape out the back. I walk around the building to the parking lot, making sure Richard sees me leave. All I find around the back is a production person on a smoke break. I ask him if he thinks Marty is going to leave out the front or the back. He's really nice, and says he'll go check with his boss. He walks up to the back door where, much to my dismay, there's Richard, who shouts, *There she is!* as if I've just committed grand larceny or something. In the meantime, my new friend, the smoker, has found his boss and lets me know that Marty will likely leave from the front. So, off I go, around the outside of the building, back to the front of the conference center.

Eagle Eye Richard easily beats me to the registration area. I casually stroll over and check in with Felicity again. No luck. She can't help me. I think for a moment. *No problem! I'll just wait until Marty comes out.*

Next thing I know a man approaches me and asks if he can help me. Eagle Eye is still there, but has stepped aside. *Absolutely, I'd love your help. And you are…?* Head of security for the company. I'm deflated. All I want to do is match a name with a face and schedule a time to follow up. I've matched a name with a face alright, but it's not the one I was hoping for.

Needless to say, I don't meet Marty. I feel horrible. I was so close. I think what bothers me the most is not that I haven't gotten to meet Marty, but that I've gone about it the wrong way. I've been so eager to leverage an opportunity that I've neglected to heed my own advice about referrals. I know better!

4.5

One day, I'll be able to share this story with Marty in person, obviously through a referral. Maybe we'll have a laugh or two. Until then, rest assured, his crack team is certainly shielding him from the rest of the world, and possibly many other potential opportunities.

Smart networkers work hard to steer clear of these common mistakes. They learn, as I did, through committing mistakes themselves or from watching others commit them. Maybe it's leaving an event realizing that the only people you spoke with were the people you already knew. Maybe you got stuck with someone who did the proverbial show up and throw up. Either way, awareness is a wonderful thing. Just being conscious of these mistakes should make you less likely to commit them. If you do find yourself in the middle of one of these situations, hopefully you can course correct and stop yourself from heading down the wrong path before it's too late.

4.5

The Networked Organization Action Plan

- Don't hang out at events with people you already know.

- Don't make assumptions about other people's networks.

- Don't ask, *How can I help you?*

- Don't make it all about yourself.

- Don't forget to follow up.

- Don't make inaccurate assumptions
  about the value of job seekers.

- Don't walk around with a frown.

- Don't forget that a referral is always better than a cold call.

4.5

Maximizing Networked Relationships

RELEVANT
NETWORKERS

Anyone can do your job, right? Fortunately, the organization has picked you to do it. How are you going to be a greater asset to the organization? What can you do to be a better steward of the organization? A networked organization understands relevancy. Its employees are constantly striving to build and maintain relevancy.

What does it take to be relevant to your team and your organization?

Are you doing the job or are you doing the job...

AND THEN SOME?

What if you and every other employee knew your organization's target customers and key offerings and were actively pursuing relationships based on that knowledge? How valuable would all of you be?

How much do you really know about your potential customers? And what about their customers? Aside from your job responsibilities, how much do you contribute to the organization? Are you just doing the job or are you doing the job...and then some?

Whatever your role may be, your *and then some* ought to have you thinking hard about what else you could be doing to help your organization thrive.

People want to work with people who understand their business. What are you doing to better understand the overall business and bring greater value to your organization? What additional value are you bringing to your company by knowing the competitors, the people, the trends, and the practices? What additional value are you bringing by connecting with people and identifying potential prospects?

Think about consultants who come in and help organizations. Good consultants are those who understand your business. The most valuable ones are those who can offer insight as to what the best practices are among other players, not only in the industry, but in other organizations with similar business models.

Think about your functional area and what's on the cutting edge. How much time are you taking to learn that skill? How much time are you taking to learn any new skill (like networking)? You just might find that what you've done for the past five to 10 years is less relevant than what you're about to do for the next five to 10 weeks.

5.1

Be relevant to your co-workers.

You probably know your team members, but what about other people in the organization?

Do you understand other people's roles and responsibilities? Do you understand what drives them and how they are measured? Do you understand how your policies and procedures affect them? Do they affect your co-workers in a positive or negative way? How often do you seek to understand?

I know a corporate finance team that takes off the last two weeks of the year. Basically, they're not available to process any sales orders through the end of the year. How would you feel if you were running sales for that organization? How would you feel if you were a salesperson counting on a few deals to come through that could make or break your commission? Would you feel as if everyone were contributing to the team? How would you feel if you were the finance team? Pretty relaxed, probably. But when you get back into the office in early January, you're probably wondering why some people in the organization aren't pleasant to you upon your return. Heck, you just affected their livelihood. How do you expect them to treat you?

Again, how do the decisions you make affect others in the organization?

I remember when I ran marketing for a technology consulting firm. It was truly the best marketing team ever! In building the corporate intranet, we developed a lot of really cool applications that enabled efficiency for the employees. One day, I received a call from the finance team, which was trying to automate expense reports… finally. They asked the technology department if it could build an application. The technology team came back and said it would take six months and cost about $100,000. Finance wondered if marketing could do anything.

Being a user of our cumbersome expense process, I was thrilled that finance wanted to work with us. How long would it take? About two to three weeks. How much? Just my team's resources and that's a sunk cost. Two and a half weeks later, we delivered a very solid expense report application accessible through our intranet that was easy to use and had integration into all of the key systems finance required. That was just the beginning of the marketing department becoming the application center of the company. We built a pipeline tracking system for sales. We built a vacation tracking system for human resources. If it could be automated, we could build it.

Things like this made our team far more valuable to the rest of the organization. Were they on our list of responsibilities? No. Did it help build our clout in the organization? Absolutely. Was the technology team mad at us? Pretty much.

When I organized the marketing team, I made sure we had a point person who would manage relationships with each function and location in the company. Obviously, each marketing team member was responsible for multiple groups, but tactics like this ensured we were in the know with what was going on throughout the organization. And it paid off. We were in the know. Oh, did I mention that our team was the only corporate team not based at the corporate office? We were almost 2,500 miles away.

5.1

What are you doing to tap into all areas of the organization? What are you doing in your organization to encourage and cultivate communication and deeper relationships? How are you aligning your team to become a conduit for better collaboration and communication across the organization? How are you aligning your team and your team's activities to become a greater asset to the organization?

What are you doing to be more relevant to your organization?

5.1

The Networked Organization Action Plan

- Understand who your organization's customer is.
- Think about your "and then some."
- Ensure your processes work for others in the organization.
- Cultivate deeper relationships in your organization.

5.1

It's All About the Attitude

Go big or go home!

I was speaking at a conference and asked the attendees if they enjoyed networking. One man raised his hand. *I can't stand it*, he said. *It's boring. I don't meet interesting people. Frankly, I'd rather stay home.* I thought about it for a second. *Ever consider that maybe the problem is not the networking?* I asked. *That maybe the problem is you? Maybe the other attendees would rather you stay home as well.* There was silence in the room for a moment.

> Maybe meeting
> **INTERESTING**
> people is about
> **WHO YOU ARE**
> when you are in the room.

Sounds a bit harsh, I know. But I mean, really, what were this man's expectations? How was his attitude delivering on his expectations?

Most people I know who enjoy networking like it because they meet interesting people. But maybe meeting interesting people is not about who else is in the room.

Maybe meeting interesting people is about who *you* are when *you* are in the room. Maybe the energy you put into networking is the energy you get out of it. Having the right attitude means going big or going home!

If every event you attend is a snoozer, perhaps that's the energy you're bringing to the table. And if every event is a home run—where you meet fascinating people, build great relationships, and find ways to help others—then you're probably bringing a different level of energy to the table.

As you know, I constantly meet really interesting people on airplanes. My seatmates usually say things like, *This flight was too short. I wanted to keep talking to you.* And I did, too! But here's the thing. I bring the energy of my love for traveling with me every time I board a plane. Of course I'm going to meet some great people. I'm excited to be there. I'm enthused about the idea of leaving one place and ending up in another. I'm excited about the opportunity to make a new friend, build a new relationship, learn a thing or two about someone else's business. And, hopefully, offer up an idea, lead, or contact, and pave the way for the foundation of a new relationship.

Maybe this is the lesson. Maybe meeting people at networking functions—whether on an airplane, at a business event, the grocery store, or even the Friday night high-school football game—isn't a function of the function, but a function of your attitude, your energy, and how much you actually bring to the party.

So, next time you're faced with an opportunity to network, do us all a favor. Go big or go home!

5.2

Feeding negative energy

Let's talk about that attitude and the energy around you. Good news travels fast. Bad news travels faster. We all know that it is so much easier and more interesting to play into the bad news, the gossip. But here's what happens.

When you tell a negative story, you give that negative energy life. When you tell it again and again, you give it more and more life. Eventually, that negative energy consumes you and is a bigger part of you than it needs to be.

I'd love to share an example of my own, but I don't want to breathe new life into any old negativity.

Instead, I'll share a friend's story. We'll call him Adam. Adam took over a new department at work and found all kinds of things wrong. In fact, so much was wrong that it was hard to find something right. Adam not only told me about the situation, but I happened to be in the room when he repeated the story to two other people. Then, at another event, I heard him repeat the story to three new people. That's when I started to think, *Wow, he really likes telling this story.* Every time he tells the story, he gets worked up about it. This story is all-consuming. This story is not positive. It's eventually going to take him over. And all Adam is going to be known for is that negative story. He'd better come up with something new, exciting, and positive. Soon!

Just because you're hired to fix the problems doesn't mean everyone in the organization wants to hear about the problems. Keep that in mind the next time you're about to relay everything that's wrong with the organization. Just like an effective performance review, with every one thing you find wrong, you better find three things that are right.

When I was in training at IBM, they had a session on feeding negativity. They talked about the Complain Train. It was easy to get a ticket for the Complain Train. Climbing aboard was even easier. The more people who boarded the Complain Train, the more it was fueled and the faster it went. The lesson there was not only to never board the Complain Train, but to never even buy a ticket! It's a difficult practice to live by because complaining is easy. And people want an ear when they start whining. But there's nothing positive about complaining and it doesn't serve anyone.

We all have bad things that happen to us. That's just life. If you're going to dwell on it, you won't be much fun. Every story has two sides. Every glass can be half empty or half full. The more you exude positive energy, the more you'll attract others who are positive. Without being too Pollyanna-ish, there's a silver lining to every black cloud. Why not spend your energy looking for that silver lining? Why not end every note of negative conversation with *The good news is…*. And don't think there's not a good side to every bad side, because there is. Sometimes you just have to dig a little deeper to find it.

This reminds me of a great book called *The Art of Possibility.* In it, husband and wife team Benjamin Zander, former conductor for the Boston Philharmonic Orchestra, and Rosamund Stone Zander, a psychotherapist, talk about the powerful role the notion of possibility can play in every aspect of life. It's an inspiring and motivational read to remind us that anything and everything is possible. The only thing standing in your way could quite possibly be you.

5.2

Take Tony for instance.

Tony is a pilot for United Airlines. Tony is responsible for the pilot grievance center, for lack of a better term. Tony decides to change this. Instead of focusing on all of the problems the pilots have, Tony decides to look for bright spots. Tony scours the organization to see not what is wrong, but what is right. Tony thinks that if he can replicate more of what's right, the *what's wrong* will begin to minimize. And that's exactly what happens. As time goes on, more and more people begin seeing the good and what is possible versus the bad.

This is exactly what award-winning *National Geographic* photographer DeWitt Jones conveys in a short film called *Celebrate What's Right With the World*. Jones talks of a time when he'd gone out to shoot a big field of dandelions. When he didn't feel the setting was just right, he left. The next day, he went back only to find the dandelions had turned into a bunch of puffballs. Could Jones have packed up his gear and called it a day? Sure. But instead, he remained open to the possibility that maybe, just maybe, he'd be able to find one great shot. And look what he got.

5.2

Yes. A puffball. But not just any puffball. A puffball signifying new beginnings and hope with light, energy, and startling beauty.

The vision that changed DeWitt Jones' life was not photographic or technical in nature, but one of attitude…a vision inspired by his choice to see the possibilities that were only there because he believed they were there.

Do you choose to see possibilities? Do you choose to believe they're there?

People like to be with people who see the possibilities, who are positive, who don't complain, and have what my yoga teacher calls an *attitude of gratitude*. Why not appreciate all that life has given you, from the friendships and the accolades to the defeats, and with them, the lessons that have followed. Why not approach every day with that attitude? Have faith in the possibilities and opportunities, and know that good things happen when you expect them to and you apply yourself.

Networking curveballs

Sure, life throws us curveballs. Then what? I was at a yoga retreat. It was incredible. One entire weekend of practicing yoga, talking about yoga, and thinking about how it positively affects our lives. During one of the sessions, Sumit, my teacher, talked about the concept of fight or flight, our survival instinct. He explained that other than choosing fight or flight, we, as humans, actually have another possibility in our bag of tricks: we have the ability to *witness*.

5.2

My interpretation of this is the ability to react, respond, or release (partly because the alliteration makes it sound much cooler).

This idea makes me think a lot about how people react to unexpected change; how people respond to adverse situations. I can tell you right now that most people are not doing a very good job. And it's affecting their attitudes. Their lives. Their relationships.

Imagine that you're on the freeway, and someone cuts you off. What do you do? Do you react by honking your horn? Do you respond by cutting them off? Or, do you do something entirely different, something entirely out of character for many drivers? Do you release it? Just let it go?

Think about it. What would happen if you didn't react? Didn't honk your horn? What would happen if you didn't respond? Didn't try to cut them off? What would happen if you calmly accepted and released the energy of the situation and then moved forward to your destination…in peace? Here's the fact of the matter: You don't have to let it get the better of you.

Remember that book *Don't Sweat the Small Stuff…and it's all small stuff*? Well, it's true. It truly is all small stuff. I mean, really, we're not all curing cancer here. Except my friend, Dan. He's trying to. But the rest of us, probably not so much. We live in a world of minor inconvenience. We also live in a world where some people make a major event out of everything. And, in turn, have a negative effect on others.

What makes one person more capable of dealing with difficult or unexpected situations? What gives one person the ability to shrug things off, while another hits the roof at the slightest irritation?

Maybe it's simply choosing to stay positive. Maybe it's having gone through adverse situations. Maybe it's about resetting expectations, about having gratitude, about being detached from specific outcomes.

5.2

We live in a stressed-out world. We're all trying to get there yesterday. We're trying to do too many things at once. We're trying to finish the game before we ever start. We're so caught up. So caught up in reacting and responding that it drives us and everyone around us crazy.

Here is my challenge to you. Next time you're confronted with a difficult situation, an unexpected challenge, be aware of your actions. Fight the urge to react. Fight the urge to respond. See what you can do to release it. Let it go. See what happens. I bet you'll find yourself in a much more peaceful and happy place. The more you do this, the easier it gets. It truly is a learned skill. The more you practice learning it, the better off you'll be, in the form of a better attitude, a better life, and better relationships!

Realizing Molly's Networking Rule #5

Assume positive intent.

Being positive has the effect of bringing about a general positive attitude. Assuming positive intent on the part of others helps move in that direction, too.

Remember our discussion about email? While most people write emails with positive intent, most people read emails assuming negative intent. Don't be like most people. Start reading the emails you receive with a sense of positive intent. You might see the same old conversations in a new light. One that makes it easier to have a positive attitude.

Assuming positive intent actually helps you be more rational. You're less likely to get defensive or create issues that don't exist. You're more likely to hear things you might not otherwise. Why?

5.2

Because you're operating from a place of trust, not skepticism or defensiveness.

In his book *The Speed of Trust*, Stephen M. R. Covey talks about earning trust and extending trust. To have trust-based relationships, you have to do your part to earn other people's trust. But you also have to do your fair share of extending trust. If you're walking around waiting for everyone to earn your trust, building relationships might take a while. To really have those trusted relationships, you have to be willing to have faith in others. To trust others.

The same goes for respect. For some reason, most people believe they ought to be automatically respected. Yet they are quick to insist that it's up to others to earn theirs. Why do they expect respect out of the gate and expect that everyone else in the organization, or on earth, has to earn it? How is that fair? Like trust, why not be worthy of respect? Earn it, but also extend it.

Realizing Molly's Networking Rule #6

Attitude is everything.

When you focus on possibilities and not constraints, it shows. When you operate from a place of positive intent, it shows. When you extend trust and respect to others, it shows. When you have a positive attitude, it shows. And conversely, when you have a negative attitude, it shows. It's much easier to build strong, trusted relationships with a positive attitude than a negative one. It's your choice. You make that choice every single day. Do you want to make it the best day of the rest of your life? It's your choice.

5.2

Choose wisely.

The Networked Organization Action Plan

- Look for bright spots.
- Assume positive intent.
- Earn and extend trust.
- Earn and extend respect.

5.2

5.3

LET THEM WIN

Let them win.

I talked about the concept of "letting them win" at the beginning of this book. *Letting them win* sounds easy in theory, but is probably the most difficult aspect of building and sustaining relationships.

The idea of letting someone win can confuse people because it seems to contradict what we believe are good conversational skills. Generally, people think of a conversation as a two-way interaction. You say a bit, then I say a bit, then you say more, and so on. But here's the problem. Just as you're sharing an experience you had, I begin thinking about my own experience and can't wait to jump in and tell you all about it. *Letting them win* is all about practicing the art of refraining from adding your own vignette or story. Why would you want to refrain? Because let me tell you what it's like to be on the other side of that story. It feels like you're trying to trump me, to one-up me. Logically, you may think you're contributing to the conversation or interaction, but you're actually taking away from it. Bit by bit. Piece by piece. You probably don't even realize

5.3

it. Most people don't. And, nobody ever tells you that you're not letting them win, because they're not even sure what this means. The result, though, is that they feel as if you're not listening to them. And, you're probably not. You're more concerned with what you're about to say versus what you just heard. The truth is that we all know it when we see it—or, more accurately, we know it when we feel it. And now that you're aware of this concept, you'll recognize it for what it is a lot more often than you could possibly imagine.

One day, I was talking to a friend. *How are you doing?* she asked. *I'm really tired,* I replied. *I was on six different planes and in three different hotels in three days.* I took a breath, then started, *Still, it was....* But before I could get out another word, my friend interrupted me. Soon she was telling me how tired *she* was. She'd taken over the conversation before I could even close my mouth. You see, she had just spent a long weekend trying to pack and get ready for a big move. She went on for 10 minutes about this big move. I got even more tired listening to her.

I'm reminded of this every day—that people are conversation stealers. Without thinking twice, they simply take over the conversation; make it about them, their needs, their ideas, their lives. They think they're adding to it, but they're not. They're stealing from it...from its value, its ability to form a deeper relationship.

To be a good networker, you need to *let them win.* Practice letting other people own the conversation. Let it be theirs. It sounds simple, but it can be difficult to do. Honestly, I used to be a conversation thief all the time until I learned this concept.

5.3

For example, my conversations around food would go something like this:

> John: *I had the best ice cream the other day.*
>
> Molly: *Oh, no, the best ice cream is in Red Square in Moscow. The ice cream person comes around about 4pm and everybody buys it. It's amazing!*
>
> John: *Wow, this is the best hot chocolate.*
>
> Molly: *Oh, no! The absolute BEST hot chocolate is in Paris—right in Montmartre where all of the artists are painting portraits. It is simply the best.*

I kept one-upping people, and I didn't even realize I was doing it. Here I thought I was adding to the conversation, but in reality, I was taking away from it. It wasn't that I had an *"I can top that and it's all about me"* attitude. I genuinely thought I was contributing to the conversation. And, in essence, I was. But it turns out that from the other side, it looked a lot like I was making it all about me.

This happens all the time in personal conversations, but it also happens all the time in business and in networking. People open things up with a question, but then take it right back by making it all about them, which makes it really difficult to take the relationship further.

You're probably thinking that the mere definition of a conversation is a two-way interaction. And yes, you're absolutely right. I have two thoughts for you, though. First, stealing the conversation brings it down to a one-way monologue. Secondly, in all relationships, there has to be some give and take. First, practice the give. Then practice the give-and-take.

5.3

Before you decide to *add* to your next conversation, why don't you wait a few minutes? Hold back. Bite your tongue. Why don't you see if the conversation can stand on its own without contributing in a way that could possibly move the spotlight onto you?

I used to have a friend (operative words being "used to") who was a constant conversation thief. It was always all about her. I'd bring up an outfit I bought and she'd follow it up with the 15 outfits she'd recently purchased. I'd start to talk about a trip I was going to take, and for the next 30 minutes I'd get the play-by-play of every trip she ever took. Everything had to be about her. It's not that I was looking for everything to be about me. It's just that if I asked, she answered. If she asked, she answered. If you asked, she answered.

Here's what I do now. When someone wants to steal the conversation, I let them have it. I don't care. That's right. I've stopped caring that I get my story in. Because networking and building a relationship is *not about me*. It's about them. If what they have to say is so important to them, then let them say it. Who cares? Remember the wise words from Dale Carnegie: *The more people talk about themselves, the more they'll like you.* The more they like you, the more they want to help you. So, at the end of the day, who cares that you didn't get to chime in with your story about your ascent of Mt. Everest? Who cares?

I was speaking at a conference and talking about this very subject of stealing the conversation. When Melea had introduced the first speaker, Reggie, she'd commented that he had called her the day before, worried that his flight wouldn't make it on time. Fortunately, everything went according to schedule, but that comment got me thinking.

5.3

When I got up to speak, I relayed to the audience how a conversation with Reggie might go if I were a conversation thief.

Reggie, I might say, *I hear your flight almost didn't make it*. Then, before Reggie would even have the chance to answer, I would delve into my story. *Well, let me tell you what happened to me. Yesterday, I got to the airport just in time to learn that my 11:15 am flight from Denver to Tampa was cancelled. The best they could do was put me on a 10 pm flight that would have connected, and gotten me to the conference at 11 am the next day, about an hour after I was due to go on stage! The ticket agent looked at all kinds of possibilities. Connect through Chicago? No, no seats. Connect through Houston? No seats. How about San Francisco or Los Angeles? No, nothing there.*

Finally I pulled out my iPad and started searching for options myself. What about this one? Denver to Birmingham, Alabama, change airlines and fly to Charlotte, North Carolina. From Charlotte, stay on that other airline and fly to Tampa? The agent worked her magic, and got me on the flights. But now, I had less than 30 minutes to get from the ticket counter, through security, on the train, and hustle through three moving sidewalks to the very last gate on the concourse before my flight departed. I grabbed my ticket and ran as fast as I could. I made it with five minutes to spare…. So, Reggie, you were saying your flight was delayed?

Here, I not only one-upped Reggie, but at least five-upped him. I trumped him like nobody's business. I might have felt great sharing that story. But I can guarantee that Reggie would feel as if I'd taken the floor right out from underneath him.

There is a difference between friendship and networking. With friends, there are times when you need the floor and times when they need the floor. If my friends call me, I assume they must have something to say, something they need or want to discuss. Then the floor is theirs, and they can have all they need. If I call them, I talk about what I need to talk about, but I also make sure we talk about them, too.

On the other hand, when you're at work or networking and still building the foundations of a relationship, you're probably not at that two-way street stage yet. So quit being a conversation thief. Yes, it's likely, no one will ever accuse you of it. Instead, they'll simply stop engaging.

The next time someone tells you how tired he is, don't take it as a free ride to tell him how tired you are. The next time someone says she's busy, don't grab the baton and give busier back. The next time someone is laid up with the flu, don't take it as an opportunity to talk about your last bout with the flu. The next time someone tells you about a big deal she's landed, don't steal the show with your bigger deal. The next time someone tells you about an interview he got, don't steal his glory by talking about the time you were in a job search. Let it be his. Let it be hers. Let them have the sympathy or the accolades.

Let them win. By letting them win, you'll be amazed how much further you can take the relationship.

The Networked Organization Action Plan

- Let them win!
- Let them win!!
- Let them win!!!

Putting the Networked Organization into Action

One day I am riding my bike. I pull into the middle of the intersection to make a left turn. When I ride my bike, I do it with the assumption that drivers are paying attention. I assume they're not talking on the phone, texting, or yelling at their kids in the back seat. I assume they're paying as much attention to the road as I am.

My bad.

As the traffic goes rushing by on both sides, I suddenly begin feeling more than a little exposed. What if someone in one of the many cars around me isn't paying attention? What if someone changing lanes causes another car to swerve uncontrollably into the middle of the intersection? What if that car comes careening toward me? What then? What if everyone around me isn't nearly as attentive as I give them credit for?

Seriously. Is anyone else paying attention?

When I sit in meetings, I usually assume people are paying attention the same way I assume drivers are paying attention to the road. I assume my colleagues are as involved and focused as I am. I assume they're paying just as much attention to others as they want others to pay attention to them. But now I'm thinking this assumption might be pretty far off.

Don't get me wrong. I'm as guilty as the next person of not always giving my undivided attention. But if you want to get good at networking, at connecting, at identifying opportunities, you need to start paying attention more closely. You need to start paying attention to the people you meet at networking functions. To the people you meet on airplanes. To the people you meet standing in line. You need to be incredibly interested in their careers, their families, their lives, their stories. You need to listen attentively. And through listening, you'll be able to identify opportunities. It might be an opportunity for you or your organization, or perhaps an opportunity to make a new friend. It could be a chance to help out someone else.

What if we stopped what we were doing and started paying attention?

Opportunity is all around us. What if the biggest opportunity of all is simply paying attention? Because without taking the time to pay attention, it's really difficult to figure out how to leverage an opportunity you're allowing to fly right by.

Oh, and speaking of flying right by, next time you see someone riding her bike, please make that extra effort to pay attention to the road, the other drivers, and her safety. She'll appreciate it more than you know!

5.4

What's in it for you?

If you want to build better relationships and create a more Networked Organization, you need to get comfortable with the idea of being in the moment. Being present. Paying attention. Being aware of your surroundings. When you master those things, you won't have to pretend you're enjoying yourself. You will enjoy yourself.

Remember, building relationships is about focusing on the other person. It's an unselfish act of actively listening to the other person. Of figuring out what you can do to help them; what you're doing to build your value in the relationship. Is it a lead, a contact, an idea? What's in it for them?

At some point or another, someone always asks me, *What's in it for me, Molly?* My answer is always the same: Everything. With the right relationships, you can do anything. The right relationships expand your thinking. The right relationships expand your personal growth. The right relationships open doors. The right relationships expand your opportunities and horizons. So, create them. Develop them. Share them. And enjoy them. And most of all, keep up the networking!

Putting The Networked Organization into action

Those executives who've been through my job networking meetings know there comes a time when I need to give really explicit instructions, like, *Write that down. Now.* And then I just sit there until you do.

This is the time for that same type of directive. It's not the time to finish the book, put it back on the shelf and say I'll get back to it.

5.4

No. It's time to set a plan. Now! Decide today that you're going to change your team, division, or organization. Decide today that you're going to begin taking action and create a culture of networking to increase collaboration, performance and revenue.

So here's what you need to do. Go back and re-read the entire book. Just kidding.

Here are some ideas:

- Have everyone in your organization read this book.
- Map out your relationships as a team and identify where the gaps are, both internally and externally. Take special note of who knows whom at your organization's target customers.
- Instead of an annual development plan for each employee that nobody looks at but once a year, have each team create a Networking Plan that is presented and reported on at the team level monthly. Doing this at the team level will provide support, encouragement and the ability to share ideas.
- Set goals for each team. Compare plans across departments. Create some friendly, fun competition.
- Create a recognition program that rewards behavior worthy of The Networked Organization.
- Get your training department involved. Have sessions on each chapter.
- Integrate the concepts and theme of *The Networked Organization* and creating a culture of networking into everything you do, including annual conferences, your corporate intranet, recognition events, team meetings, and recruiting.

5.4

If you still don't know what to do, just call me. We can talk about how to get started.

For every day that passes by, your organization is missing out on the opportunity for better collaboration, authentic relationships, and accelerated revenue.

The opportunity to become The Networked Organization.

It's a bold idea. Are you bold enough to embrace it?

5.4

ADDENDUM

ADD

Molly's 7 Hard-and-Fast Rules of Networking

RULE 1 ········▶ The Golden Rule: Networking is not about you

RULE 2 ········▶ Build the well before you need the water

RULE 3 ········▶ Be there and aware

RULE 4 ········▶ Be interesting by being interested

RULE 5 ········▶ Assume positive intent

RULE 6 ········▶ Attitude is everything

RULE 7 ········▶ Let them win

ADD

Relationships Based on the Five Forces (pg 81)

Competitor	Supplier	Buyer/ Customer	Substitute/ Complementary Product & Service

Begin by mapping out your direct competitors, suppliers, buyers, and substitutes. Write down the people you know in each area. Identify people who provide complementary products or services to your customer. Figure out where the gaps are. Develop a plan to forge new relationships in those areas.

ADD

Relationships by Functional Area (pg 83)

ADD

Name	Company	Date Met	GM	Ops	Fin	Sales	Mktg	HR	SC	Eng	IT	Legal

Map out who you know. Fill in the gaps with who's missing. Mark existing relationships with an X. Mark desired relationships with an O. Utilize those with an X, and others in your network, to get referred into those with an O.

Relationships by Business Model Template (pg 87)

Name	Company						

Map out who you know. Fill in the gaps with who's missing. Mark existing relationships with an X. Mark desired relationships with an O. Utilize those with an X, and others in your network, to get referred into those with an O.

ADD

335

Market Leadership/Corporate Social Branding Alignment (pg 103)

Market Discipline	CSB Key Messages	Ideas/Examples that align with your CSB
Operational efficiency	The numbers; the results	
Customer service	The human component/ solving the customer's problem	
Product excellence	Product innovation, the latest and greatest	

ADD

Major Sporting/Entertainment Events (pg 146)

January	College Football Bowl Games (Major Bowls), College National Championship, NFL playoffs, NFL Pro Bowl, Australian Open Tennis Tournament; Golden Globes Award Show, Oscar Nominations, Consumer Electronics Show
February	Super Bowl, Winter Olympics (every 4 years), the Oscars, New TV shows debut
March	College Basketball March Madness Tournament, NIT Tournament, Major League Baseball Spring Training, the GRAMMY Awards
April	MLB Opening Day, NFL Draft, NBA Playoffs, the Master's Golf Tournament
May	NBA Championship, French Open Tennis Tournament, Kentucky Derby Horse Race, Preakness Horse Race (2nd leg of the Triple Crown)
June	U.S. Open Golf Tournament, NHL Stanley Cup Finals, Wimbledon Tennis Tournament, World Cup Soccer (every 4 years), Tour de France Cycling Championship, Belmont Stakes (last leg of the Triple Crown), Internet of Things Conference
July	MLB All Star Game, Summer Olympics (every 4 years)
August	NFL Preseason, College Football Season begins, U.S. Open Tennis Tournament
September	MLB Playoffs, Ryder Cup Golf Tournament, New TV shows debut
October	NHL Season Opener, MLB World Series
November	NBA Season Opener, Elections
December	College Football Bowl Games (Minor Bowls), NFL end of regular season

MLB – Major League Baseball
NHL – National Hockey League

NFL – National Football League
NBA – National Basketball Association

ADD

Questions That Start Relationships (pg 243)

Purpose	Goal	Types of Questions
Networking Events	Break the ice. Find out who they know. Get them to like you so they'll open up their network to you.	• General in nature • Non-threatening • Conversation openers
One-on-one	Learn about the person/company/industry. Find out who they know. Get them to like you so they'll open up their network to you.	• Specific/relevant • Inquisitive • Borderline bold
The Interview	Learn about the company strategy. Determine if it aligns with your objectives. Get them to like you and to think you're the right person for the job.	• Thought-provoking • Strategic • Bold
The Airplane	Break the ice. Learn about the person/company/industry. Find out who they know. Get them to like you so they'll open up their network to you.	• General in nature • Non-threatening • Conversation openers
Conferences	Break the ice. Learn about the person/company/industry. Get them to like you so they'll open up and share their insights.	• General in nature • Non-threatening • Conversation openers

ADD

Molly's Top 7 "Back Pocket" Questions
(pg 244)

When a networking opportunity presents itself, don't forget the questions you should keep in your back pocket:

1. *What do you do?*
2. *Who do you work for?*
3. *How long have you been there?*
4. *And where were you before that?*
5. *And how long were you there?*
6. *And where were you before that?*
7. *And how long were you there?*

ADD

Questions into the Future (pg 248)

Today	5 to 10 Years in the Future
Who are your customers today?	Which customers will you be serving in the future?
Who are your competitors today?	Who will be your competitors in the future?
What is the basis for your competitive advantage?	What will be the basis for your competitive advantage in the future?
What skills/capabilities make you unique today?	What skills or capabilities will make you unique in the future?

Ideas for Putting
The Networked Organization into Action

- Have everyone in your organization read this book.

- Map out your relationships as a team and identify where the gaps are, both internally and externally. Take special note of who knows whom at your organization's target customers.

- Instead of an annual development plan for each employee that nobody looks at but once a year, have each team create a Networking Plan that is presented and reported on at the team level monthly. Doing this at the team level will provide support, encouragement and the ability to share ideas.

- Set goals for each team. Compare plans across departments. Create some friendly, fun competition.

- Create a recognition program that rewards behavior worthy of The Networked Organization.

- Get your training department involved. Have sessions on each chapter.

- Integrate the concepts and theme of *The Networked Organization* and creating a culture of networking into everything you do, including annual conferences, your corporate intranet, recognition events, team meetings, and recruiting.

ADD

The Networked Organization Action Plans

Section 1.3: Building a Networked Organization from the Inside Out

- Pick up the phone! Next time you're about to send an email, pick up the phone and have a conversation instead.
- When you see an email that you read negatively, call that person for clarification.
- Set up meetings with five people from different departments with whom you don't normally interact.
- Onboard new employees with a personalized networking schedule. Include what each person does and potential areas of focus for the conversation.

Section 1.4: The 7 Hard-and-Fast Rules of Networking

- Networking is not about you.
- Build the well before you need the water.
- Be there and aware.
- Be interesting by being interested.
- Assume positive intent.
- Attitude is everything.
- Let them win!

Section 2.1: The Intentional Network: Building Your Relationship Portfolio

- Identify 20 people you'd like in your network: Company, Function, Industry, Business Model (five in each).
- Capture information in an online CRM tool, Excel spreadsheet, or on paper.

ADD

- Develop your questions to gain a better understanding of that functional area, industry, or business model.
- Make an effort to connect other people to each other.

Section 2.2: Networking through Social Media and "Corporate Social Branding"

- Create/Modify LinkedIn profile.
- Create your own authentic social network by inviting a couple of new connections per week.
- Contact at least one person per week to say hello, see what they're up to, and figure out how you can help them.
- Before connecting with someone, ask yourself the following questions:
  - *Who is this person?*
  - *Have I ever met him/her in person before?*
  - *How do I know him/her?*
  - *Am I confident that having this person in my network will be a positive reflection of me?*
- Develop a co-branding strategy with your employees.

Section 3.1: Networking: That First Impression

- Get business cards instead of giving business cards.
- Master the handshake.
- Develop your basic intro; think of stories/examples.
- Download NetNotes from mollywendell.com.

Section 3.2: Networking Events

- It's not about you. It's about them.
  Ask questions to get them talking.
- Don't give cards; get cards.

ADD

343

- It only takes one good contact to make a networking event a success.
- Be the good. Figure out how you can help others.

Section 3.3: Networking at 30,000 Feet

- Networking is about everyone but you. The more you ask, the more you learn.
- Select your seat carefully.
- Find the fascinating in everyone you meet.
- A good networking conversation rarely consists of your doing any of the conversing.
- Avoid drinking alcohol at networking events, including on airplanes.

Section 3.4: Networking at Trade Shows and Conferences

- Engage other attendees in a conversational, questioning style.
- Remember that booth workers often know people who could be of value to you. Get to know the booth workers.
- Use this as an opener: *So, what are you finding of greatest value at this conference/event/trade show?*
- Create a goal of meeting and providing value to at least five people at every conference or trade show.
- Head to the edges at loud parties and be cautious about your alcohol consumption.
- Make personal hygiene, e.g., having fresh breath with no dry mouth residue, a priority.

ADD

Section 3.5: The Networking Dinner (or Lunch)

- Schedule a dinner party. Ten is the ideal number to have at dinner. Have more to invite? Do two dinner parties.
- Choose your invitees with forethought on how they will contribute to building relationships among the attendees.
- Assign seating to ensure there is good opportunity for mingling. Spouses/partners should be seated apart from each other.
- For lunches, a smaller number, as few as two plus you, works.
- Let people know they're paying for their own lunch.
- End your invite with *Would you like to be included?* Everyone likes to be included.

Section 3.6: Networking Referrals

- Get referrals, not introductions.
- Take inventory of your organizations'"true" social sphere of influence and build programs to leverage it.
- Create a group of like-minded people.
- Enable your field service organization with relationship training and key opportunity-identification questions.
- Show people you're referral worthy.

Section 4.1: Extending Networked Relationships: Getting a Meeting

- Avoid cold calling by getting referrals.
- Use Molly's renowned Call/Call/Email Approach.
- Schedule the meeting for a time that's mutually convenient.
- Remember, the onus is on you to make the meeting worth their time.

ADD

Section 4.2: Smart Networking Questions

- Develop your set of smart questions.
- Show you're a good listener by taking good notes.
- Give, give, give before you ever think of getting.
- It is your responsibility to keep the conversation moving.
- Don't ask, *How can I help you?*

Section 4.3: Networking Follow-up Guide

- It's never too late to follow up.
- Perfect the art of the Thank-YOU letter.
- Be sure your interactions are positive ones for all involved.
- Never make assumptions about why someone hasn't responded.
- Relationships are not built in a day, but over a lifetime.

Section 4.4: Networking Etiquette

- Take notes old school style—with a pen and paper.
- In your emails, put action items in the first line.
- Make sure the signature and Reply To line in your email has the same contact information as your business card.
- Personalize your phone greeting.
- Think about how you introduce people; make it personal and relevant.
- Do your research.

Section 4.5: The 7 Essential Secrets of Smart Networkers

- Don't hang out at events with people you already know.
- Don't make assumptions about other people's networks.

ADD

- Don't ask, *How can I help you?*
- Don't make it all about yourself.
- Don't forget to follow up.
- Don't make inaccurate assumptions about the value of job seekers.
- Don't walk around with a frown.
- Don't forget that a referral is always better than a cold call.

Section 5.1: Relevant Networkers

- Understand who your organization's customer is.
- Think about your "and then some."
- Ensure your processes work for others in the organization.
- Cultivate deeper relationships in your organization.

Section 5.2: It's All About the Attitude

- Look for bright spots.
- Assume positive intent.
- Earn and extend trust.
- Earn and extend respect.

Section 5.3: Let Them Win

- Let them win!
- Let them win!!
- Let them win!!!

ADD

REFERENCES

Carlson, Richard. *Don't Sweat the Small Stuff.* Hachette Books, 1996.

Carnegie, Dale. *How to Win Friends and Influence People.* Simon and Schuster, 1936.

Covey, Stephen. *7 Habits of Highly Effective People.* Simon and Schuster, 1989.

Covey, Stephen M. R. and Merrill, Rebecca. *The Speed of Trust.* Free Press, 2006.

Ferrazzi, Keith. *Never Eat Alone.* Doubleday, 2005.

Gladwell, Malcolm. *Outliers.* Little, Brown and Company, 2008.

Gladwell, Malcolm. *The Tipping Point.* Little, Brown and Company, 2002.

Hamel, Gary and Prahalad, C. K. *Competing For the Future.* Harvard Business Review Press,1996.

Heath, Chip and Heath, Dan. *Made to Stick.* Random House, 2007.

Jones, Dewitt. *Celebrate What's Right with the World.* Star Thrower Distribution, 1996.

Porter, Michael. *Competitive Strategy.* Free Press, 1998.

Treacy, Michael and Wiersema, Fred. *The Discipline of Market Leaders.* Addison-Wesley Publishing Company, 1995.

Wendell, Molly. *The New Job Search.* North Audley Media, 2009.

Zander, Benjamin and Stone Zander, Rosamund. *The Art of Possibility.* Penguin Books, 2000.